My Thanks

Jennifer Macedo was a very kind, sweet girl who I knew back in High School (Go Whalers!). We were never more than friends, but she was the very first person I ever showed any of my stories to. I used to keep them in notebooks hidden in the back of my closet. I was your typical fat, near sighted nerd and my stories were way too personal to expose to actual criticism.

When I mentioned I liked to write she begged to read some of my stories. She told me she really loved them and that I should always write. Hearing that meant a lot to me, and I promised her that if I ever wrote a book I would dedicate it to her. We lost touch after High School and I have no idea where she is now or if she will ever read this.

But promise kept.

Kelly Kilroy is my best friend. He is the sort of friend who will tell you you're being an idiot when no one else will. He will also listen when you really need to talk. I once quit a dead end job and moved down to Florida with him because he told me, 'I need a roommate and I know you won't steal from me.' He gave me a whole lot of crap at times, but he also gave me a lot of good advice that I wish I had taken. While he didn't specifically help me with writing, he has helped me more than any single person outside of my parents. He has always been there when I needed him and is everything a best friend should be.

And Kelly, if you're reading this:

"Hey, who are you? What are you doing? Get out of my garden!"

Mistress Winowyll, and no, that's not her real name. She has been with me throughout the writing process. Acting as a Beta, giving me story ideas, yelling at me when writer's block had me stumped, and helping me write some of the scenes. She also pointed out things I would have missed completely due to being the author. Writers have a peculiar blindness because we know everything about our stories and make assumptions that the reader won't. Luckily I have her to illuminate the blind spots and give me the truth when I need to hear it. Or when it will give her a good laugh at my expense. She also keeps promising to step on me later. Did I mention I both love and fear her?

Chapter 1

A Good Master

Waldo had kept them running through the woods all night.

His wand in hand, he kept warning them that they might be attacked at any moment. His familiar / wife / succubus Alice needed no further encouragement. Waldo's more recently acquired familiar / ogre Gronk was more inquisitive.

"What are we running from?" he asked in an airy, lisping voice that did not seem to belong to his hulking body.

"My grandfather," Waldo said.

"We're running away from your grandfather?" Gronk asked. "Is he that scary?"

"His grandfather is an archlich, who can use lightning bolts and other powerful magics," Alice said.

"He has sworn to chase me to the ends of the world until he eats my heart," Waldo added.

"What did you do? Steal his candy?"

"I didn't do anything. Apparently family blood just tastes better."

XXX

Waldo and his two familiars got as far away from the city of Middleton as they could. When the sky lightened, and the horrible ball of fire began to rise over the horizon, they finally halted. Waldo dropped to his knees panting. Alice and Gronk were breathing a little hard but remained on their feet. They were somewhere in the woods, well off any road.

"We got away," Waldo said between breaths. "The protective wards worked."

"So maybe he won't ever find us again?" Alice asked.

"That would be too much to hope for. The wards can block scrying and detection magic, but there are other ways to track someone."

"Wonderful."

"We will deal with that later. Right now let's get some sleep."

"Sounds good," Gronk said with a wide smile, two yellow tusks jutting from his lower lip. The ogre was hugging himself and twisting from side to side. "Be gentle with me."

Alice placed herself between Waldo and Gronk and crossed her arms. "Don't get any weird ideas."

"Oh, don't be that way pretty girl. I'm okay with sharing."

"There is not going to be any sharing! He is my husband, and I am the only one who gets to sleep with him. You sleep a safe distance from us."

"Awwww, but he's my master. Shouldn't he get to use my body, too?"

Alice suddenly snatched Waldo up and was shoving his face into her bosom. "No sharing! Mine! Got that?"

"Alice... you're... crush... ing... me."

"Oops, sorry darling, sorry." She immediately released him.

His legs were unsteady, but Waldo managed to stay on his feet.

This is what I get for messing up the contracts. Waldo thought.

Waldo was a mage, and both Alice and Gronk were his familiars, bound to him by magical contract. Thanks to the binding ritual he had performed on each of them, Waldo had a special bond that allowed him to sense their strong emotions, always know their location, and gave him the ability to summon them with a single word of magic.

However, the contract should have also forced both of them to obey his every command and made it impossible for them to physically assault him. That was most definitely not the case. Waldo had somehow botched the ritual both times and made it only partially effective. Alice and Gronk were both able to ignore his orders and touch, or even hit and kick, him as they pleased. That left Waldo no choice but to act with more care than a master normally did.

"Gronk, now that we have stopped and actually have a chance to talk, there is something I would like to discuss with you."

"What is it, master?"

"All right, first off why are you talking like that? When we met you sounded the way I would expect an ogre to. 'Gronk like pretty man. Gronk no do.' Why are you speaking with a lisp and using adverbs and adjectives?"

"I don't know. It just comes naturally to me, I suppose."

"Then, why didn't you talk that way from the beginning?"

The eight-foot tall ogre shrugged. "Old owner like when Gronk talk this way. Make Gronk sound like dumb ogre." He switched back to his high pitched, lisping voice. "I can tell you're much more refined, master."

Waldo shut his eyes and pinched the bridge of his nose. He would have been happier with a typical brute of an ogre, too. Though, with the contract being defective, a regular ogre might have decided to spit him over a fire and peel off his skin for a snack.

"The way you talk isn't the real problem here." Alice clutched one of Waldo's arms. "What was the idea of kissing him before?"

Gronk stuck his tongue out. "Don't be jealous 'cause he likes me better. He kissed me first, and it made my knees weak."

Waldo could feel a little vomit in his mouth. "When I kissed you, it was just the final part of the binding ritual. Also, my kiss was chaste. I didn't put my tongue down your throat."

"I just couldn't help myself. You were just so forceful!"

"Huh?"

Gronk was hugging himself and twisting from side to side again. "You were just being all manly and dominant. I just couldn't control myself."

Waldo shook his head. "You really are gay, aren't you?"

"As a cabin boy on a six month ocean voyage."

"You're gay?" Alice asked. "You actually want to do *that* with men not women? That is sick and unnatural!" Despite being a succubus and having been brought up in a house of ill repute, Alice had some very conservative ideas about sex and how men and women should relate.

"Afraid I can give him something you can't?"

Alice's lips peeled back as she let out a low growl. Without intending to, her body was quivering, and she was on the verge of transforming into her true form.

"I don't have any issue with homosexuality," Waldo said quickly. He put a comforting hand on her shoulder. The last thing he needed right now was for the two of them to fight.

At his touch Alice calmed a bit.

"I am not gay, though, Gronk. I am not even bisexual. I am only interested in women."

Alice turned her head and raised a single fiery eyebrow. "By that you mean you are only interested in me, right husband?"

You really would expect a succubus to be more open minded. "I do not plan to ever have sex with anyone who is not my wife."

That brought a satisfied nod from Alice. Waldo meant what he had just said, but the words didn't have quite the meaning Alice thought.

"That's disappointing," Gronk said. "Especially after you went and got me all excited like you did. Well maybe that can change."

"*No, it won't,*" Waldo and Alice said in the same breath.

"Cute," Gronk giggled.

"Listen, Gronk," Alice said. "There is something you need to know. Waldo is not what he appears to be. He isn't a White Mage at all. He is actually a Dark Mage. You understand what that means, right?"

Gronk's eyes widened. "Is that true, master?"

Waldo nodded. He was dressed in dirtied but still white robes. "Yes, I am a Dark Mage from Alteroth. I came here on a quest, and you will serve me and help me fulfill its requirements."

"So that means you know all about torture and inflicting pain on people, right, master?"

Waldo nodded. "I do, but so long as you obey me…"

"That's great! I'm so lucky! Please do whatever you want with me, master, I am a sub who has been searching for his dom."

"Oh," Waldo said without enthusiasm. "I see."

Alice looked from Waldo to Gronk and back again. "Uhm, what are you talking about?"

"Gronk is a submissive," Waldo said.

"A what?"

"I like to be punished and disciplined," Gronk said with a playful wink. "Please punish me, master. Gronk has been bad."

Alice stared at the ogre and then shook her head. "I don't understand."

"Gronk is what is referred to as a submissive or a masochist." Waldo explained. "To put it simply, he enjoys pain and being humiliated or dominated."

Alice's mouth twisted. "You *enjoy* getting beaten and shamed? What sort of freak are you?"

"The submissive sort. Weren't you listening, sweetie?"

Alice turned back to Waldo. "And how do you know about this?"

"Some of the slaves enjoyed that sort of thing. I remember we had this one burly laborer from Rutenia named Gregor. He always wanted to have red hot pokers shoved into…"

"Stop! Stop!" She was waving her hands about. "I do not want to hear this!"

"Then, why did you ask?"

"So will you discipline me, master, and do all sorts of cruel and wicked things to your servant?"

Waldo thought for a moment and then shrugged. "If you like."

Gronk almost swooned. "Joy."

"Are you being serious?" Alice demanded.

"I am willing to make certain sacrifices to keep both of you happy."

"So you really are into torture?"

"I am not 'into' it. I have never enjoyed it or actually practiced it on anyone, but growing up where I did you pick up the basics."

"Please do whatever you like with your servant." Gronk started pushing his index fingers together and digging his toe into the ground. "Could we do the 'Clawing Eagle'?"

"That's a bit advanced, and we don't have a rack or even chains."

Yanking his arm, Alice began dragging him away. "Waldo and I are going to have a nice long chat and then get some sleep, way over there. You stay right here."

Waldo was stumbling and trying not to fall as Alice kept his arm in a vice like grip. "You're angry."

"How'd you ever guess?"

XXX

As he watched, Gronk laughed to himself. "Well, I can see who the sub in that pair is."

Chapter 2

Troubled

Lilith Corpselover was troubled.

She stood before her bedroom mirror. There was no reflection to be seen, only a gray formless mist. Lilith had been trying to look upon her son Waldo to see if he was safe. Scrying magic was among the most difficult to master. It worked best when the subject was someone you knew and had a strong connection to. Being an elite archmage, trying to spy on her precious son had never been a problem before.

A week ago she had watched as her boy got himself in trouble with his familiar Alice over a misunderstanding about his relationship with his sister Gwendolyn. There had been no issue calling up his image. Since the following morning, she had not been able to look upon him, no matter how she tried to rework the spell.

Lilith chewed at her lower lip. Something must have happened during that night. The only thing that could block her attempts at viewing would be some sort of protective ward. Waldo was very skilled at those, and it would not be hard for him to block all magical efforts to scry or detect.

"But why would he suddenly do that?"

Something must have happened. Unfortunately, there was no way for her to find out what. Even for an archmage, there were limits to what you could do. Protective wards would normally defeat the effect of any sort of spell, except when it was used from very nearby. Lilith took comfort from just one thing: her son was definitely still alive. The effects of a ward used on living flesh were always temporary. Wards cast on inanimate objects were permanent; on the living they would vanish within a day or the moment the caster died. The mere fact her efforts were being blocked meant Waldo was alive.

Lilith Corpselover was head of one of the seven ruling families of Alteroth. Waldo was her last living child and designated heir. Four of her other children were dead and two were mostly dead. The other ruling families had conspired to send her son out on a First Quest with almost impossible conditions. They considered Waldo weak and more of a White Mage than a Dark one. Everyone assumed Waldo could never succeed in completing the quest and so would never return. Lilith was alone in her belief that he would succeed and come home one day.

Waving a hand she brought the spell to an end. The mist vanished, and she could once more see her reflection. It was frustrating not knowing what Waldo was doing, but she would keep her faith in him. She had set plans in motion that would secure his position when he eventually returned. Lilith would just have to concentrate on those and trust that Waldo would manage.

"Stay safe my son."

Lucius Corpselover was troubled.

The archlich held a crystal ball in its withered hand. There was nothing to be seen other than a formless gray mist.

"Well, it's not as if I were expecting anything different."

It had been a little over a week since their encounter. Lucius had come after his last surviving grandson expecting to have a little bit of fun before devouring the boy's heart. The archlich had known Waldo's reputation as a weakling and had not expected much of a fight. The fact the boy had actually trapped him inside of a containment circle and survived had come as a huge surprise.

Lucius had been pleased.

Being mostly dead, existence tended to be rather boring. Dealing with an actual challenge was an absolute delight! The archlich had sworn to track down and devour not only Waldo, but his little succubus, too.

"*Nunc.*" The mist vanished and the crystal ball was once more clear. The archlich slid it into one of the pockets of his robe.

"I can't blame you for using protective wards to hide from me," Lucius said to himself. "But I think I have been patient long enough."

Taking out a wand, the archlich began to draw a circle in the ground surrounded by various runes and magical symbols.

"If I cannot track you myself, then I will just summon something to do it for me."

Melissa Cornwall was troubled.

The cause of her trouble could be defined with just two words: Waldo Rabbit.

Her confrontation with him had been a complete and unmitigated disaster. She had tracked him down intending to recover some stolen property and then execute him. Being a White Mage and an archmage, she had been confident in her ability to deal with one criminal. That had been her undoing. He had managed to trick her and get her to swallow some love potion.

Melissa had realized what he had done, but it had not helped. Even being aware it was an illusion, she had not been able to fight her feelings of love. She had willingly handed him her wand, purse, and spellbook. Melissa had stood there and waved as he escaped the city with his wife and newly purchased ogre.

Now it was the following morning, and she was in her quarters in the Baron's palace in Middleton. She was without funds and without her wand or spellbook. Fortunately, she still had a number of spells memorized. A member of the Order of Mist was never truly alone. Melissa bolted the door. She had already informed the palace staff that she would be spending the entire day in meditation and was not to be disturbed for any reason, including meals.

Standing in the center of the room, Melissa breathed slowly and readied herself. The deeper magics could be very difficult some times. She concentrated on the incantation as well as on the hand gestures. The more complex the spell, the easier it was to make a mistake, and the more dangerous mistakes could be.

When she was at last certain, she raised both hands with thumbs and forefingers pressed to palms. She began to move them in an intricate pattern as she spoke her spell.

"Avarnos est lidado ibi loco esto sempre ako notarmos loco deste."

The instant the last syllable was spoken and her hands completed the final gesture, she felt the mana torn from her body. Before her eyes the room was ripped away. The world was gone, and she was staring into the void. For just this moment, she existed outside of time and space. She was not moving, rather all of creation was moving around her. If you had the ability, and knew the right spells, you could twist the universe into whatever shape you liked.

Surely, this is what it feels like to be a god, Melissa thought. It was blasphemous, but she couldn't keep herself from thinking it.

As quickly as it had gone, the world snapped back into existence around her. There was ground beneath her feet, and the smell of grass and dampness filled the air. It had been morning, but now it was pitch black. Overhead was the moon and the starry sky. All around her in the darkness were the twisted forms of soulwood trees.

She was home again. She had returned to the nation of Avalon.

Her legs trembled, and she stumbled back. Her back struck a tree trunk. Otherwise, she would have fallen to the ground. Melissa's heart was pounding, and her breath was coming out in ragged gasps. Her whole body was trembling. It was as if she had just gone ten miles at a full run.

"Good," she said between breaths. "It's good to be reminded that I am only mortal."

The teleportation spell had taken her three thousand miles in the blink of an eye. Doing so had drained most of the mana from her body and left her physically exhausted. She would need a meal and several hours rest to be able to cast it again and return to Middleton.

Through magic almost anything was possible, but there were always limits, and there was always a price. For instance, teleportation was only possible if the location was already know to you. It had to be a place you had actually been to before. It was impossible to teleport to a place you had never visited. The spell also demanded a great deal of mana, requiring more the further you wanted to travel. Mana was the magical energy used to work spells and wards and potions. Every being who could use magic had a certain amount of mana within them.

So long as you stayed well within your limit, there was usually no issue. As with physical exhaustion, you could recover lost mana naturally with rest and sleep. Use up too much at once, and you would feel the effects. Your body weakened, and you felt weary, just as though you'd run for a long distance or spent hours at a strenuous task. You might be unable to work other spells, and it was possible to lose consciousness and be unable to wake for hours.

Mages who used too much mana constantly risked damaging their bodies and shortening their lifespans. Go past the body's limit and death was a real possibility.

Melissa pressed her back to the snow white tree. Her legs quivered, and she had to make an effort just to remain on her feet. Melissa shut her eyes and just breathed.

It always does this to me. It always takes near everything I have.

It was humbling, but perhaps all magic users needed to be humbled now and again.

XXX

It took about twenty minutes before she felt strong enough to stand on her own. Putting one foot in front of the other, she slowly began to exit the grove. Though it was nighttime, she was able to cautiously navigate her way through the trees. She needed to duck a couple times to avoid some of the low lying branches. She caught her foot on a root hidden by the thick grass.

The soulwoods were important symbols to Melissa and members of her Order. According to legend, they held the souls of mages who had been killed during the Shattering. The anguished faces made from knots in the wood and the twisted and deformed shape of the trees themselves were said to be because of all the evil that plagued the world. One day, when the world was purified, the trees would grow tall and straight without a single deformity.

Until that day they would be a constant reminder of their noble struggle.

XXX

The grove was located about three miles from the capital. For reasons of security, no one was permitted to teleport directly into the city. As she made her way cautiously along the road, Melissa could make out the humble cottages that lined the way. Simple homes constructed of wood and straw. Each one was neatly kept with a small garden out in front. The residents were all yeoman farm families, who owned their own small plots of land and lived tranquil lives.

Melissa could have walked up to any one of those homes and likely found the door unlocked.

The thought made Melissa hold her head up a bit higher despite her weariness. Avalon was paradise on earth. All the monsters had been hunted to extinction centuries before. There were no bandits and virtually no crime; the penalties were harsh and ruthlessly enforced. The local nobility followed a strict code of chivalry, and served, "The One We Follow." Nobles acted as the local magistrates and authorities but were not permitted to abuse their positions. They were held even more strictly to account than the people were. Unlike most of the world, here in Avalon there really was only one law, and all men and women were equal before it.

In the Misty Isle, people could live without fear.

The nations of the Alliance were not quite so tranquil. They still had banditry and crime. Many of their rulers only paid lip service to the idea of equality before the law. But at least their lands were no longer infested by monsters. Year by year and generation by generation, the Alliance states would become more and more like Avalon.

It doesn't matter how slow the progress is, Melissa thought. *No matter how many lifetimes it takes, we will succeed.*

Her travels had shown her how corrupt most of the world was. Good, decent, hardworking people were forced to live in perpetual fear. Not only from monsters but from criminals and from lords who cared more about fleecing them than about protecting them. The more she saw of the world, the more certain she became of the righteousness of her cause. The land cried out for Unity, Justice, and Peace.

XXX

By the time she arrived at the outskirts of the capital dawn was breaking, and the city was stirring awake.

Simple wood framed homes and shops pressed together around a tangle of roads and streets. The city had been no more than a village back before the Shattering. Over the last two thousand years it had grown organically. The main thoroughfares had cobblestones, but most of the roads were still dirt. The city blocks were of different sizes, the streets twisted and curved, and the businesses were scattered about.

Camelot could be a confusing place to those not familiar with it.

At the very heart of the city was the ancient castle that had given this place its name. Long ago, after the world had been shattered and fallen into chaos, a great king had fought and unified the lands of this isle. He was the first to serve The One We Follow and to espouse the philosophy of Unity, Justice, and Peace. The castle was his seat and the home of his royal court. When Avalon became a single nation, it became the capitol.

The castle itself was impressive. Its outer wall was fifty feet high and twenty feet thick, with walkways and battlements running all along its four sides. Go through its single gate, and you would find a small courtyard and a great citadel. The citadel was actually no less than five separate buildings, all connected by covered walkways. The central and oldest building was a modest three story fortress. It was simply a solid block of granite with a basic design. Two of the other buildings were towers, each rising more than a hundred feet and going far above the outer wall. The towers were wide at the base and grew progressively smaller, with both ending in pointed rooftops of polished bronze. The remaining two buildings were squat and bulky by comparison. They had enormous archways and ribbed vaults, as well as carved statues and vast panes of stained glass. The towers gave one a sense of freedom and possibility, whereas the cathedrals were meant to humble and awe. All the buildings were interconnected; you could enter any one and then visit all the rest without having to ever step outside.

The ancient castle was the home of the three orders that ruled Avalon in the name of The One We Follow. The Order of Mist, which Melissa belonged to, was based within the two towers. The Order of Virtue, to which every knight and nobleman was a member, controlled one of the cathedrals. The Order of the Faithful, made up of the priests and clergy, held the other cathedral. The original Citadel was shared by all three.

The orders were united by their faith and the desire to bring salvation to the rest of the world. They did frequently disagree as to the best method. These little differences were always kept quiet. To both the faithful and the wicked, Avalon would always appear united and strong.

XXX

Walking through the streets of Camelot, folk were only beginning to come out. Everyone Melissa saw had eyes of yellow. The shades ranged from gold to ripe wheat to honey. It was physical proof that they were all one people.

When they spotted her, no one tried to keep their distance. There were no fearful stares. They all smiled and waved to her.

"Blessings," people called out.

"Blessings unto you, as well," Melissa answered.

Children ran to her. A couple of little girls gave her daisies which she happily accepted. In Camelot and the rest of Avalon, White Mages were seen as benevolent guardians. They maintained the peace and enforced the laws. They healed the sick and made the rains fall. They kept the protective mists about the island that only allowed those who had been invited to pass through. They enforced order, both in nature and in society. The people trusted them, as children should trust their parents.

It had been a long time since she had felt so welcomed.

Eventually she arrived at the heart of the city and was passed through the gate into the castle. Melissa went directly to the Tower of the Moon. Within, fellow mages, acolytes, and servants all politely greeted her as they went about their daily routines. She went to the fifth floor where the Great Library was. It actually took up the fifth through the ninth floors. As Melissa had known he would be, Minister Barrows was there. He was not only a Minister but also held the position of Keeper of Knowledge, which made him responsible not only for the books and tomes of the library, but also for the agents set out to gather information.

In less civilized nations, he might have been called a spymaster.

As soon as he spotted her, his golden eyes widened. He gave no other sign of being startled, though.

"Mistress Cornwall," he said in a perfectly neutral voice. "I had not expected your return for another three years. May I ask you what brings you home so suddenly?"

Melissa curtsied to him. "Minister Barrows, I am afraid I am in need of aid."

"The Order will always take care of its own. What assistance do you require?"

She chewed the inside of her cheeks, then forced herself to look him in the eye as she spoke. "I have lost my spellbook, my wand, and all my gold."

Melissa stood there, head up and back straight, ready to accept whatever lecture he chose to give her. For a mage to lose her spellbook and her wand was not merely humiliating, it smacked of gross incompetence.

Instead he simply gave a slight nod. "I will draw funds from the treasury and provide you a virgin wand. I can have the scribes copy more advanced spells and add them to an acolyte's spellbook. I am familiar with your abilities and can guess the spells most useful to you."

She felt relief that he was not asking her the reason she found herself in these circumstances.

"I look forward to reading your report on your most recent activities. I expect it to be in my hands before you depart, of course."

There was a sour taste in her mouth. "Yes, Minister."

"Tell me, did you succeed with recruiting the mage Roger from Bittford?"

"No, Minister, and I am afraid I will have to set that aside for the time being. There is something far more important which requires all my efforts."

Barrows raised an eyebrow. "And what might that be?"

"I am going on a rabbit hunt."

Chapter 3

Politics as Usual

It was early morning, and Lilith was in one of the vacant rooms near the top of the south tower.

"Incorpus."

With a single word of magic, she summoned one of her creations. On the stone window sill was a black bird with empty eye sockets. It stared at her lifelessly, patiently awaiting its master's command.

Lilith placed a single finger atop the thing's head.

"I have transferred the necessary funds and made them available to you. Make the purchases that you require. I wish you every success in your noble endeavor." She withdrew the finger and made a shooing motion with her hand. "Go. Deliver the message."

The bird hopped about and spread its wings. It took off and was quickly lost in the charcoal skies. It would not stop until it had reached its intended recipient. The creature would speak the words in its master's voice and then disintegrate and turn to ash. If, for whatever reason, it were captured or brought down before reaching its target, it would destroy itself. For delivering messages to non-magic users, her little pets were ideal.

One more small step.

If any of the other families discovered what she was doing, they would turn on her. No doubt they would believe she had gone mad. For these endeavors secrecy was absolutely vital. Even Hera and Enver had no idea what she was about. The only other person who knew her plans was Gwendolyn, and being a ghost, her daughter was unlikely to share her secrets.

Well, not unless she got too bored.

The task complete Lilith headed downstairs to go to breakfast.

XXX

In the grand dining hall was a single extended table. There were forty chairs, all evenly spaced along both sides. Only four of them had place settings; one lay at the very head of the table, one to the immediate right, and two to the left. The space to the right would remain empty, the plate, goblet, utensils, and napkins would be left untouched until the servants cleared them away.

In the first seat to the left was a zombie in tattered black robes. There was no plate or goblet or utensils in front of it, merely a silver tray. It fidgeted, and the clawed fingertips of its right hand drummed on the table. As Lilith strode across the hall, its milky white eyes locked on and followed her.

In the second seat was a young woman with a hideous nose. She wore a cream colored blouse and skirt made of silk, with embroidery in gold thread. The girl was leaned back with her hands folded on her lap.

"I hope I did not keep you waiting too long." Lilith motioned to the servants as she took her place at the head of the table. They bowed in acknowledgement and hurried into the kitchen to fetch the food that was already prepared.

"Not at all," her apprentice Hera said. Her son Walter, the zombie, gave a grunt. Hera sent him a sharp look but said nothing.

Lilith pretended not to notice. She had spent an hour last night reattaching one of Walter's arms following his "introduction" to Hera. He had demanded over and over again that Hera be punished for attacking him.

"I want her dead! I want her dead!" he'd shrilled like some spoiled child.

Lilith had answered him with a single sentence. "If you kill her I will not punish you."

That had finally silenced him.

The servants brought out bowls and trays filled with fresh bread, fruit, wheat cakes, eggs, and slices of meat. One of them served a chicken, not pieces or a whole cooked chicken. The bird had only recently been strangled and was still whole, it had not even been plucked. The servant placed the fowl down on the tray in front of Walter.

Grabbing the bird with both hands, Walter brought the meal up to its mouth. Short pointed teeth tore into its neck and ripped the head clean off, spattering blood and causing it to drip down onto the table and floor. Walter noisily began chewing the head, feathers, beak and all.

Hera was just beginning to spread some butter on her bread as she was forced to watch the vile display. "Must you do that?"

Swallowing what was in his mouth, Walter grinned at her. There was a bit of blood dribbling down his chin a couple feathers stuck in his teeth. "If it bothers you don't look." Walter leaned forward and tore off another chunk of the bird, squeezing as he did so, deliberately causing more blood to squirt.

"Disgusting!" Hera said. "My father has pigs that are better mannered than you!"

"I'll bet they're prettier, too."

Hera's hands turned into fists, and her shoulders hunched. Her right hand went beneath table, obviously reaching for a wand hidden in a fold of her clothes.

Lilith rapped the table with a sharp knock and drew their attention. "There will be none of that in my presence. I will not have you using your wand or casting magic in my company without permission."

Hera swiftly put her hand back on the table and bowed her head. "Yes, Aunt Lilith."

Walter had a wide smile. "That should teach you your place."

"Of course," Lilith continued. "What you do outside of my presence does not concern me."

Walter sent his mother a betrayed look.

Hera was suddenly the one smiling.

They are like a pair of squabbling two year olds, Lilith thought.

"Mother, you cannot mean that!"

"You know better," Lilith said. "Only children need their parents to protect them. Once you put on the robes, you must be strong enough to defend yourself."

If it were possible, the zombie looked ill. It dropped the mangled chicken on the tray and rose to its feet. "If you will excuse me, mother, I think I will go."

She gave him a nod. "As you wish."

"I will see you soon," Hera said. There was an eager look in her eye.

Walter withdrew as quickly as he could.

Though Lilith gave no outward sign, she was pleased. Walter had been growing arrogant of late. Her son had needed a reminder of his place.

"That really was revolting." Hera snapped her fingers at the closest servant. "Remove this mess and bring me fresh bread."

The man immediately moved to obey.

"Remain where you are," Lilith said.

The servant halted.

"It seems Walter is not the only one who is being presumptuous this morning. You can have the servants do whatever you please when I am not about. However, when I am here, I am the only one who will give them orders."

In her seat Hera offered a hasty bow. "Forgive me, Aunt Lilith. I was just trying to be helpful."

"That dress you are wearing. Did you bring it with you?"

Hera remained perfectly still and composed. "No."

"Where did you obtain it, then?"

"I told the servants to bring me clothes and other things I might need."

"I see. It might interest you to know I recognize the clothes you have on. They once belonged to my daughter Kara. She has been dead eleven years."

"If I overstepped my bounds, I apologize, Aunt Lilith. I arrived here with only my robes and small clothes. I assumed my needs would all be provided for. I can return the clothes and have my father send me my wardrobe and other things."

She is very calm, Lilith thought. *The only time she loses her composure is when she is angry.*

Lilith waved a hand dismissively. "Keep them, along with whatever else you have acquired. But remember you are not my daughter yet, only my apprentice. You keep your position at my whim. Do not forget that, niece."

"Yes, Aunt Lilith."

"Oh, and you are not to destroy Walter."

Both of Hera's thin eyebrows rose. "But just now…"

"Walter required a lesson. There is a limit to how much I will put up with. Yet zombie or not, Walter is still my son. I would not be pleased to see my son destroyed."

"I understand." Hera paused. "Can I at least punish him?"

Lilith nodded. "Certainly, though zombies cannot feel pain, so it may not be as satisfying as you hope."

Hera shrugged. "I will take what I can get."

Lilith waved to the same servant to clear away the remains of Walter's meal. She and Hera then settled down and had a peaceful breakfast.

The meal was nearly done when her steward Hollister entered the dining hall and strode quickly to Lilith's side. She knew immediately that something must have happened. Hollister bowed low to her. "Mistress, we have just received a message requesting a meeting of the Council of Seven within the hour."

Unscheduled meetings were always about bad news. No one ever called for one to announce the birth of a healthy child or the creation of a new spell. "Who has requested this meeting?"

"The message came from Darius Heartless, mistress."

"Wonderful, just wonderful. Well go and prepare my escort."

"Yes, mistress." Hollister bowed once more and swiftly departed.

"It seems your morning lessons will have to be cancelled, let us hope the interruption is short."

"Does this happen regularly, Aunt Lilith? You seem to be taking this very calmly."

"It occurs from time to time, though, Dark Powers be praised, not often."

"Are you not at least curious as to the reason?"

"I already know what this will be about. Darius would only call for a meeting if it somehow involved Avalon. The only question is how severe is the problem."

XXX

Lilith waited half an hour before setting out with her escort. That was deliberate on her part. She liked being the last to arrive. It gave the others the impression they were waiting for her to begin. Appearances were very important. For instance, the Council Hall was an impressive looking building. In the city of Alter, only the castles of the ruling families could compare to it. Many considered the Hall the most imposing building in all Alteroth.

That Hall was built completely of black stone and was in the shape of seven discs, each one stacked upon the other and each slightly smaller than the one below. Every block of stone had been warded to provide both security and protection from attack. Hundreds of thousands of blocks had been used in construction, it represented a staggering amount of magic. When anyone arrived in Alter their eyes were always drawn here first. The height and shape of the building were unique, and being the home to the Council of Seven gave it gravitas.

In reality, almost every room above the first floor was empty. Except when it was actually being used for meetings, it served mainly as a residence for the slaves who worked there and a place for storage. A much smaller building would have served just as well.

But the real purpose of the Council Hall wasn't simply to hold their meetings. It was to *impress*, and it did so wonderfully. Its imposing grandeur was impossible to miss or ignore, and that sense of majesty was reflected on the Council and the Seven Houses that formed it. So what did it matter if the rooms inside were gathering dust?

Lilith could well appreciate how important image was. Very often, what appeared to be true was more important than what really was. One of the reasons her son had been forced to go on his quest was because she had not bothered to protect his reputation. She could have. It would have been difficult, but she might have put on fake demonstrations and spread false rumors. Perhaps even forced her other children to support her claims. Making people believe Waldo was a powerful mage would have been a challenge but not impossible.

At the time, though, Lilith had still had her other children, all of whom looked to be more likely candidates to succeed her. Had she given Waldo such blatant favoritism, the others might have seen him as a threat. He likely would have had an accident as soon as he put on his robes. Lilith had also believed shame would motivate him. It was never her way to be soft with her children. The world was cruel, and each of them needed to be strong enough to find a place in it.

By the time the situation had changed and it was clear Waldo would have to be her heir, the damage was done and there was no repairing it. The Council had not wanted a weakling to replace her and had forced Waldo on his nearly impossible First Quest. In turn it led her, with Gwendolyn's aid, to come up with her rather drastic plan to ensure his survival if… *when* he returned. Taking on Hera as her apprentice, so that she could one day marry Waldo and help guide him, was just one small aspect of her scheme. The message sent out this morning was another. Many other wheels would begin to turn soon.

Plots within plots, wheels within wheels, I will burn it all down if I must.

XXX

As expected, she was the last to arrive. Her usual seat was empty and awaiting her. An unexpected change caught her attention as soon as she entered the inner chamber. Tiberius Blackwater had exchanged seats with Xilos Soulbreaker and was now sitting to Darius' right. The two of them had their heads together and were having an animated discussion. Darius had his hands flying about as he spoke, while the younger Tiberius gave an occasional nod and comment. Gawreth Wormwood was watching with a stern countenance, not surprising given that he and Darius had been feuding for years.

Lilith was certain the other members had also noted the sudden shift. If the Heartless and Blackwater families were drawing closer, it represented an important alteration in power. Tiberius was new to his position as head of the Blackwater family, and he was a completely unknown entity. Was he serious about tying himself to Darius? Was this simply for show? Once again the importance of appearances came to mind.

As soon as she took her seat, Darius rose to his feet to address them. "Now that we are all here I will share with you the horrible news." As was his habit, he was being brusque and getting directly to the point. "King Doran has closed his border to us! Our merchants and our people will not be allowed into the Kingdom of Dregal. This outrage cannot be allowed to stand!"

The words caught most of the Council members by surprise. It was common practice throughout the Shattered Lands to allow merchant caravans free access. Trade enriched all those who participated, and Alterothan merchants could be found almost everywhere. Closing a border was extremely rare and considered a great offense. In all the world, only Avalon and its puppets had ever done so.

Until now.

Right on the heels of Darius, Dante Poisondagger spoke. "I agree. Such a despicable act cannot be tolerated."

Lilith narrowed her eyes. *He has been bought.* Poisondagger was always hungry for gold, and it was no secret that his support was available to the highest bidder. She glanced about the table. *Darius has two votes, perhaps three. Does he have a fourth?* If he did, that meant Alteroth was about to go to war.

Darius nodded. "I am sure all of you feel as I do. This insult must be avenged!"

"Has Doran actually joined the Alliance?" Gawreth asked.

"Not yet," Darius scowled. "But it's obvious where his heart lies."

"If we only traded with the folk who loved, us we'd have no partners at all," Gawreth said.

The two men openly glared at one another.

Lilith found the animosity reassuring. Gawreth would not support Darius even if he put forward a motion to give children milk.

"Do we have any merchants in Dregal?" Baldwin Blooddrinker asked in his usual, regal tone. "I stopped sending caravans there three years ago, when the harassment and price gauging became too much. Do any of you have merchants there?"

Eyes glanced all around. No one spoke or raised a hand.

"Well, then," Baldwin said. "How does this change anything?"

"It changes everything!" Darius said. "It's a sign of contempt and cannot be ignored! If we let them get away with it, other countries will see us as weak!"

Tiberius Blackwater nodded. "If we do nothing, it will badly damage our reputation."

"We cannot respond to every little provocation," Gawreth said.

"You think this little?" Darius demanded. "This yellow slug of a king is telling us that we may not set foot in his worthless country. To ignore that would be cowardly. Are you a coward, Gawreth?"

Gawreth Wormwood shot to his feet.

"I agree that we must act," Lilith said. She saw surprise on Darius' face, followed swiftly by satisfaction. "We must retaliate immediately. I say we close our border to Dregal's merchants and people, as well."

"An excellent suggestion," Baldwin said. "I was leaning the same way."

Darius twisted about as though he had been stabbed. "What good would that do? None of their people are in our territory!"

"It seems the appropriate response," Lilith said.

"I agree," Gawreth sat back down. "A perfect answer."

"It makes us look weak," Dante said.

"Well, you would know all about that," Lilith said, unable to resist getting in a dig.

"As would your son."

Lilith stared at the despicable old man. That was a better retort than he usually managed.

"Closing the border is sheer stupidity!" Darius waved his arms about. "The only answer is war!"

"Your answer for everything," Gawreth said.

"Because it is the *only* answer!"

"Give it up Darius," Lilith said. "We all know what you are aiming for. You are just using this as an excuse."

Baldwin nodded. "Your true agenda is a war with Avalon and the Alliance."

"It's not like you have ever kept it a secret," Gawreth said.

"So what?" Darius slammed both hands on the table. "Why will none of you understand? We must go to war with them!"

"They are our enemies," Tiberius said.

"War seems the only answer," Dante said.

"Were this a war with Dregal alone, I think we would all support you," Baldwin said in a calm manner. "I believe we would even agree if it meant fighting all three of the northern kingdoms. Going to war when Avalon would almost certainly intervene is another matter. There is no guarantee we could defeat the Alliance, and even if we were to triumph, they are too far away for us to occupy. The best we could hope for is a costly victory which would still leave our enemies intact."

"We cannot avoid fighting them, and the longer we delay the stronger they become! Visit any court in a hundred different lands, and what will you find? White Mages spreading their lies, winning converts, and turning countries against us. Every day we do nothing they spread their poison. Now, Dregal is in their camp. Tomorrow it will be Lothas, then Wylef, and before too much longer we will be encircled by Alliance armies! Every day they grow stronger, and we grow weaker! War is inevitable, and for us the sooner the better!"

Tiberius and Dante nodded, while Lilith, Baldwin, and Gawreth looked on stonily.

Lilith glanced at Xilos Soulbreaker. He was the only member of the Council not to have spoken. Xilos simply sat passively. He had never been in favor of war with the Alliance. Had Darius brought Xilos into the war camp? It would be difficult; Xilos could not be easily bribed, and he was not new to the Council as was Tiberius.

Whether he had or not would soon be evident.

Darius put his shoulders back and lifted his chin. "I declare we should go to war with Dregal and punish their impertinence. Let the Council of Seven speak."

"I say no," Gawreth said.

"I say yes," Tiberius said.

"No," Baldwin said.

"Yes," Dante said.

"No," Lilith said.

Six sets of eyes turned to Xilos. He leaned back and chuckled. "Well, this is a rarity. I usually don't get so much attention."

"Side with me," Darius said. "Think of the spoils! All the land and slaves each of us will take."

"Consider the cost of a defeat against the whites and if the gain is worthwhile," Baldwin said.

Xilos held out both hands and alternately lifted and lowered them like scales. "You both make excellent points. If only there were something to tip the balance."

Lilith scowled. House Soulbreaker was wealthy enough and could not be easily bribed, but Xilos had no issue with twisting the situation to his advantage. It was at moments like these that Lilith wondered if their system of government might be flawed.

"Five thousand gold skulls if you vote with me," Lilith said.

"Six!" Darius said.

"Seven," Lilith said.

"I will add a thousand, as well," Baldwin said.

"So will I," Gawreth said.

It was common knowledge that Corpselover was far and away the richest of the Houses. Blooddrinker was the second.

Darius glanced to his right. Tiberius pretended not to notice. He did not even bother to look to Poisondagger. With a snort of disgust he crossed his arms and sat.

"Well, then, things are made clear." Xilos let one hand drop to the table and lifted the other past his shoulder. "I say no."

And with that war was avoided.

For the time being.

XXX

Baldwin put forward a motion to close the border with Dregal. It was passed unanimously. Knowing he would not get his declaration of war, Darius accepted this lesser alternative.

As Lilith returned home, she knew what she would teach Hera today. Her apprentice would begin to learn just how politics and government in Alteroth worked.

Chapter 4

A Stab in the Back

Skilled hands strummed strings and slapped drums, while lips played flutes and other instruments. No less than sixteen musicians stood in a corner of the hall, providing a pleasant background to the evening meal.

In a dozen silver lamps, myrrh was burning, filling the vast chamber with sweet, smoky fragrance. Three long tables were placed end to end, and eighty nine people were seated at them. There were ninety place settings and ninety chairs, but one was left deliberately open. Upon the table were whole roasted pigs, chickens, and sheep. Baked fish, as well as succulent beef and venison, were piled high. Fresh baked bread, fruit, nuts, and vegetables were there, with only the best wine to wash it all down. For dessert there would be cakes and pies and puddings. All of them served by elven maidens dressed in silks any woman would be happy to wear.

Anywhere else, such a lavish spread would be reserved for a feast day or some other special occasion. In Castle Poisondagger, this was an ordinary meal.

Celton Poisondagger was seated eighth from the head of the table on the right side. He was the firstborn of Dante Poisondagger and his first wife Cecilia. Celton was a fifty-one-year-old archmage with decades of experience in helping to run the family estates. He had been entrusted to handle many delicate matters and knew how to be both subtle and forceful. Most of his time had been spent cleaning up his father's many messes.

Celton glanced to where the musicians were playing, to the lamps giving off wisps of grayish smoke, to the elven slaves in all their beauty and splendor, and to all the delicious food weighing down the table. All he could think of was the cost of it all, the waste. After a time, the music, incense, and servants all faded into the background. Even the food and drink grew bland when every meal was a feast.

He glanced about the dining hall. More than anywhere else in the castle, this was a showplace. There were tapestries imported all the way from Trebizon, portraits and paintings commissioned from various artists, suits of armor made of silver, enchanted weapons and shields, and marble statues were to be seen all along the walls. They were all nothing more than garish displays meant to impress people with how cultured and prosperous the Poisondagger family was. It reminded Celton of a coward who bought a huge sword and then went about telling everyone about how very brave he was.

The truth was the family *should* have been doing well. They did not own any gold or silver mines, but they had plenty of land and people. In Alteroth, taxes were not paid to the central government. Each House took as much as it pleased from the slaves and serfs it controlled. The tiny fraction of free citizens were exempt. Of course it also fell on each House to maintain the roads, enforce the laws, and provide military protection in the territories they controlled. The Great Families enjoyed both the advantages and burdens that came with complete autonomy.

The Poisondaggers had as much territory as any other House. The farms and villages produced plenty of food. The towns and cities made consumer goods. All of which belonged to the family. It should have been plenty. The other families never had any financial issues.

Yet their territory was plagued by bandits, the roads were becoming unsafe, the troop levels were barely adequate, and in the last several years there had been riots. People understood what would happen to those who opposed a Great Family's will. That so many were ready to run the risk spoke volumes about how bad things were becoming. Their slaves and serfs accepted they were going to be exploited, but they would not accept being denied the essentials. Slaves needed to be fed, given shelter, and provided at least some sense of security. Even the most dimwitted apprentice knew that much.

People were beginning to go hungry, because his father had ordered more and more of his lands to be used to grow tobacco rather than food crops. In the cities and large towns, crime was becoming increasingly common, and in some, gangs were beginning to form. The police forces and garrisons were underfunded and undermanned. The incompetence and corruption of the local authorities exacerbated these problems.

The governors and overseers were all members of the extended family, relatives who felt entitled to stuff their own pockets. Every House had to deal with a certain amount of corruption, and, in general, the problem was ignored so long as it remained manageable. Due to his father's stupidity, though, the issue had grown worse over the years. In certain areas as much as half of the revenues that should have been raised disappeared without a trace. Celton had gone to these spots and had the worst offenders publicly executed as examples. This would improve the situation for a short time, but eventually greed would always overpower fear.

At the head of the table sat his father, Dante Poisondagger, patriarch of the Poisondagger family and member of the Council of Seven. Sitting to his immediate left was his ninth wife. Katrina was eighteen and younger than some of his father's grandchildren. The old man looked to have not a care in the world. He was laughing at whatever nonsense Katrina was spewing out of her penis-gobbling hole. Everyone close to the head of the table laughed as well, only too eager to try and please. His father was eating some lemon pudding. With his rotten teeth, his diet consisted only of soft foods and strong wine. He cared not at all for the business of running his House and preferred to conserve his strength for his pleasures instead.

We should have killed him years ago, Celton thought. *Then we wouldn't be in such a mess.*

Celton shifted his focus to the empty seat to his father's immediate right. A plate, goblet, and utensils had been put there, but no one was ever allowed to sit in the chair. As his father's first born son, Celton knew there were many countries where he would have been the legitimate heir. In Alteroth, however, it didn't matter who was born first. What mattered was power and reputation. The head of a family was expected to choose the candidate with the greatest ability as the successor. This normally led to fierce competition among all the contenders to prove themselves. It was a wonderful system designed to weed out the weak and reward those ruthless enough to do whatever was necessary to stand above the rest.

The person who was heir was always seated to the immediate right of the family head. The proximity of where you sat at the table was a reflection of your standing within the family. Your place was never set in stone. Yesterday, he had been seated ninth on the left side. The day before, he had been sixth on the left side, and the day before that, he had been twelfth on the right side. Within the main family, there were seven candidates to replace father, himself included. They were constantly being shifted about, as if in a game of ninepins. The chairs closest to the front were always occupied by the wives and by weaklings who were no threat to the succession. The heir's seat was always empty, and Dante made it obvious he had no intention of ever naming someone to inherit.

Celton stuffed a big chunk of beef into his mouth and chewed on it slowly. He was the first to admit his father could be very clever when he chose. It was also clear he had a well-honed survival instinct. Dante Poisondagger was seventy-three years old, and had been head of the family for forty years. He had taken a total of nine wives and fathered thirty-six children, including nineteen sons. At the table were many who wanted nothing so desperately as the old man's death.

Yet there he sat, laughing, joking, and so very full of life. Celton's father had many shortcomings but was an absolute master of self-preservation. In their world, power was everything. Family bonds, love, and loyalty all fell away when there was an opportunity to rise above the others. Position came before all else; there was no place for the weak. Every member of the family had this truth drilled into them from birth. From the moment you put on the black robes as an apprentice, you were expected to protect yourself. And if you could arrange an "accident" for a rival, so much the better.

This applied to the head of the family every bit as much as it did to everyone else. If the leader of House Poisondagger grew weak or careless, it was only right he be replaced by someone stronger. Normally every Great Family had a designated heir to make the transition smooth and (nearly) bloodless. Each head of family was expected to try and hold onto power for as long as possible, but to also make sure the person who replaced them was the best candidate available.

His father did not give a damn what happened to the family once he was gone. Dante cared only about living for as long as possible. If it meant there would be utter chaos when he breathed his last, well, the Dark Powers could sort it all out.

Celton glanced a couple spots to his right. His cousin Pyrus, an archmage, was eating quietly. A little further down was Fenwyk, another cousin and archmage, laughing loudly at everything their father said. Turning up the table on the left was his younger brother Murat, yet another archmage. His brother noticed and lifted an eyebrow. Celton turned his attention back to his plate. There were other faces he was in competition with. Only one person could become the next head of family. Everyone else would be exiled to one of the branch families living in the countryside or other cities. There was only one prize, and they were all fighting for it. Even though they all wanted father dead and gone, they couldn't conspire with each other. Celton knew anyone he talked to might, would likely, betray him to father. It would remove a competitor and earn father's temporary favor. His father had no issue ridding himself of a threat.

Trust is a dagger pointed at your own heart was a saying Celton knew very well.

"A thousand gold skulls!" His father chortled and wiped his eyes. "He paid me a thousand gold skulls and got nothing for it!"

Everyone near the head of the table laughed along with him. Each trying to laugh louder or appear more amused than anyone else.

A thousand gold coins, and how long will they last? Celton wondered. That much gold was worth two million copper knuckles, an absolute fortune. *It will probably be gone inside of a month.*

Celton did not laugh along with so many others, but he also knew better than to actually speak his thoughts out loud. If he did his father would probably seat him at the far end of the table with the grandchildren still too young to be apprenticed.

As with most of his meals Celton ate his food and said nothing.

XXX

As he made his way to his apartment, Celton passed one of his nephews in the corridor. Virgil was one of Pyrus's boys, a middling mage who specialized in evocation. His nephew gave just the slightest nod, a gesture he returned. As his nephew went by, Celton deliberately slowed his pace and turned his shoulder slightly so he could keep his eye on the young man.

He was not surprised to see Virgil do the same.

A stab in the back was the Poisondagger family motto. Living within the castle among the main family didn't mean you were safe. He knew plenty of them would be happy to get rid of him. Celton could think of a few people he would not mind ridding himself of, as well. The problem was doing it without being too obvious. Accidents were acceptable; killing someone openly was not.

Everyone in the main family had to deal with fear. It was the future that wore on nerves and left so many trying desperately to find any way to please father. Eventually the old man was going to die. Amazingly, it might be of natural causes. Since there was no designated heir, no one knew what would happen when the day came. No one was strong enough to declare themselves the next head and be certain of getting support. If you declared yourself, and the members of the family refused to acknowledge you, it would mark you as a failure and usually cause a quick and painful death.

In most of the Great Families, when someone declared him or herself the new head it was usually a mere formality. Those who might be rivals would acknowledge him because they would not have the support to risk a challenge. For anyone who was not already an archmage, it was always safer just to kneel and acknowledge the heir. Smooth successions were bloodless successions.

What occurred recently with the Blackwater family was an exception. Tiberius had not been the designated heir. He successfully removed his father and eliminated not only the proper heir but all the other potential candidates in one daring move. When Tiberius declared himself family head, the rest of the Blackwater clan acquiesced, and the Council had acknowledged an established fact.

Celton had no doubt his rivals dreamed of doing something similar. The problem was there was no trust. No one would dare conspire with anyone else for fear of being betrayed. And there were simply too many other strong mages and archmages for any single person to safely deal with.

So what would happen when his father breathed his last?

"Blood and chaos," he muttered to himself.

Celton thought of the pit fights held on the Winter Solstice. All the criminals in custody were handed a sword, pushed into a pit, and told to kill each other. They always hesitated at first, each one afraid of the rest. But then one would stab his neighbor, and they would all get the idea. The men would attack desperately, while trying to watch for those trying to come from behind. Some men would make impromptu alliances and help each other for a while. Usually those unions ended suddenly with one stabbing the other in the back. Things always wound up degenerating into a mindless frenzy without any sort of order. It was rather pointless, as the "winner" got fed to the zombies.

Celton found these matches very entertaining. He did not, however, want to actually participate in one.

He entered his room intending to relax a bit before going to bed. When he spotted a slip of folded paper on top of his pillow, he drew his wand and quickly cast a spell. He was relieved to discover there were no hidden wards or enchantments within his apartment. The door had been locked, but that meant little. Anyone with magic or a lock pick could have gotten in. Father did not allow anyone but himself to magically seal doors.

Knowing there was no magic cast into the paper, Celton picked it up and unfolded it. "If you seek glory come alone to the corner of Centaur and Amber streets at the second hour past midnight."

Glory? That was not a word of often associated with the Poisondagger family. Lies, betrayals, and conspiracies were what its members were known for. Who had time for something as pretentious as glory?

Was this a set up for an assassination? Someone wanting to draw him outside of the castle where it would be easier to get rid of him? Could it be an attempt to bring him into a plot? He did not recognize the handwriting. Pyrus, Fenwyk, Murat, Dantos, Sabot, Jovan… were one of them trying to eliminate him?

Celton looked at the piece of paper in his hand and considered.

XXX

It was the second hour and Celton was in the designated place. He had a wand in hand and was hiding against the side of one of the houses. The entire place was swallowed in darkness. There were no street lights, and every window and doorway was shut tight without so much as a flicker. The only slight illumination came from the Rivers of Fire miles away at the Forge.

Celton waited in the darkness. He was not about to cast a spell to make himself an obvious target. In the end, he had decided the potential reward outweighed the risk. If someone in the family were trying to plot father's death, he would hear them out. If the conspiracy looked promising, he might join it. Otherwise, he would inform father of it and remove an obstacle. If this were an assassination attempt, which was very possible, he would try and eliminate his rival first. Either way, Celton saw this as an opportunity to advance.

He remained as still as possible, peering into the blackness, searching for any movement. Being a magic user, he would sense the approach of any mage. He had several combat spells memorized and would not hesitate to cast at the first sign of treachery.

Celton was still staring out into the empty street in front of him when a hand suddenly grabbed hold of his throat. Another hand took hold of his right wrist, forcing him to drop his wand. He was then slammed into the wall where he had been hiding. The grip around his neck was like a vice crushing him. He choked and hacked trying to breathe. Without his wand and unable to speak or freely move his hands, he could not use magic.

In the dark, red and slitted eyes appeared before his own. Inky lips pulled back in a bloodless smile to reveal fangs.

A vampire! Celton had been outwitted after all. He expected those fangs to rip out his throat and for everything to end.

Instead, the monster spoke to him. "I take it you are Celton Poisondagger? I've already eaten, and if I wanted to kill you, you would be dead. Forgive my rudeness, but I did not want you to attack me by mistake. Do you understand?"

The iron grip loosened barely enough to let him breathe again.

"Yes," he gasped.

"Good. Now we can talk."

The vampire let go of him and casually strode a few steps away.

Celton snatched his wand from the ground and pointed it at the vampire. He had never faced one before and never realized how silent and quick they were. To say nothing of strong! This one was a few inches shorter than he was and looked positively frail. After the initial demonstration, Celton would not be fooled, though. "Who are you? No one in my family has a vampire under their control." He kept his arm steady and was ready to cast if the monster did anything threatening at all.

"I should hope not. It would be an embarrassment if one of my kind were captured by a member of your clan." The vampire performed an elaborate bow, causing the cape about his shoulders to whip about. "My name is Enver."

The name was well known. Celton sucked in a deep breath and considered killing the creature immediately. "You're Lilith Corpselover's familiar."

"I am."

"What does House Corpselover want with me?"

Enver shook his head. "Nothing. I am not here on behalf of my mistress."

"Then, why are you here?"

Enver spread his hands. "I've come here to offer you and your family the chance to get something you have wanted for a very long while."

"What do you mean?"

Enver spoke slowly, as if savoring every word. "I am offering you the chance to kill my mistress."

Chapter 5

<u>Better Than Flowers</u>

Waldo sat on the ground with the spellbook he had taken from Melissa in his lap. Having spent the entire night running, this was his first chance to go through it. Rather than studying any of the spells or recipes or wards, he was skimmed through to get an idea of what was here.

It quickly became obvious that Melissa had not been bluffing about being an archmage. There were many complex spells a mere mage would not be able to work. From the selection it was also clear Melissa was primarily skilled in wind magic. Waldo noted only four healing spells: all basic, closing cuts, removing bruises, that sort of thing. By comparison he counted thirty three separate spells using air magic, ranging from creating a simple breeze to flying to bringing down a cyclone.

I was lucky to trick her the way I did, Waldo thought. *I would have stood no chance in a fight.*

At the moment he had only one offensive spell involving rudimentary fire magic. He would definitely study some of these wind spells and try to add them to his inventory. The more advanced incantations were beyond him, but learning some of the fundamental ones might be possible. Other spells and potion formulas looked interesting as well.

With his wand in hand, he spoke a word of magic, *"Ventus."*

Wind burst from the tip of his wand. It was strong enough to rip leaves off of trees and make some branches shake and bend. Waldo nodded to himself. While not as inherently deadly as fire magic, it might be of use.

He had two spellbooks now, the one stolen from Roger and the one from Melissa. Since Melissa's had far more written in it, he would copy all the spells and formulas from Roger's and add them to hers. Even though Waldo considered most of the spells Roger had to be more or less useless, you *never* wasted magical knowledge. When the task was done Waldo, would probably try to sell Roger's spellbook. If he were lucky enough to run into a mage interested in illusion or weather magic, it would fetch a good price.

"Why am I the one setting up the tent?"

Waldo glanced up from his book. Alice had about finished getting it ready. "Who else would do it?"

Alice crossed her arms beneath her ample bosom. "Normally, a man would feel ashamed to let a woman do this sort of work for him."

"Fortunately I don't have such a problem." He immediately sensed anger and annoyance coming from her through their bond. "What? Servants are supposed to do the menial tasks."

"You are not going to start about me being a familiar again are you?"

Waldo instinctively rubbed the part of his upper right arm where she had grabbed hold of him earlier. "No, at this point I have given up on properly training you."

Alice narrowed her eyes. "I really wish you would act like a normal husband."

"I am a Dark Mage, and you are a succubus. What precisely would "normal" be for us?"

"For starters, you could not do any weird things with the ogre."

"So you want me to only do the weird things with you?" Alice's cheeks grew rosy, and he could sense a surge of embarrassment. "A bit selfish isn't it?"

"Since when is it selfish for a wife to want her husband to be faithful to her?"

Her indignity made him chuckle. "You have never been to Alteroth."

"This is Lothas. Whatever sorts of laws you grew up with don't apply here."

"So? After we collect my third monster, we'll be leaving. I haven't decided where we'll go yet, but I expect we will have to do a lot of traveling. Do you wish me to follow the local beliefs of whatever piece of ground I happen to be on? I am Alterothan. More importantly, I am heir to the Corpselover family. Our motto is, 'We are bound by no laws.'"

Alice began shifting her weight from one foot to the other. "Does that mean you are going to do whatever you want?"

Were he a true Dark Mage, the answer to that could only be yes. "You don't need to worry. I am not gay, and I've already told you I don't intend to have sex with anyone I am not married to."

"Well, that's a relief, but are you going to do any weird stuff, though?"

"What do you consider weird?"

"Anything involving chains or ropes or red hot pokers."

"You know, Alice, succubi are considered to be the embodiment of lust... to be lust incarnate. As such, they tend to be accepting of all sorts of desires. You are probably the most close minded one walking the earth."

"Good," she planted her fists on her hips. "I'm glad that at least one of my kind is decent. Now, are you going to do those sorts of things with Gronk?"

"I don't plan to, but it is possible. Since my contract with him is defective, as it is with you, I need to make more of an effort to see he is happy in my service. Do you want a discontent ogre traveling with us?"

"Well, no, but there have to be other ways to make him like you."

Waldo shrugged. "To each his own. We all have our own wants and desires. As I have said, I don't plan to perform any torture sessions, but I won't rule out the occasional switching or light beating, if he is deserving some sort of reward."

"If I do something you like please just give me flowers."

"Actually, I would probably service you instead."

"Wh… what?"

"I mean, what we did in our room the night before last. When I was pleasuring you, and you were making all those loud noises. I could tell you were really enjoying it, especially when you kept screaming for me to go harder."

Her face was completely red. "Why are you bringing up our wedding night all of a sudden?"

"I was simply pointing out how I would reward you."

"Don't you dare pretend you didn't enjoy it, too."

"I did, but the point is you would prefer being pleasured to being given flowers. Like a ram servicing his flock, I would make sure to do my best to satisfy your needs."

"Did you just compare me to a sheep?"

"It's a metaphor. It's not meant literally."

Alice rolled her eyes. "How very noble of you, enduring such a trial all for my sake."

"Yes."

"Look, darling, I am a woman, not a mindless animal. I am happy to make love with my husband, but I don't need you to "service" me only to try and keep me happy."

"I see." Waldo closed the spellbook and stood. "I am glad you told me. I was planning to do so with you right now."

"You were?"

"Yes, it was going to be my way of thanking you for all you did to help me acquire Gronk. I was planning to take you… roughly."

"Roughly?" She echoed in a weak voice.

"Very roughly, you seemed to enjoy it. But if you prefer, I will get you some flowers instead."

Alice began to tug at her hair as her eyes avoided his. "Well…"

XXX

Gronk was lying on the grass staring up at the blue sky. Though his master's tent was more than a hundred yards away, he had no trouble making out Alice's cries.

"Yeeeeeeeessssssssss! Oooohhhhh yeeeeeeeessss! Give it to me haaaaaaaaarrrrddddeeeeeeeerrrrr!!!"

"Bitch," he sighed.

Chapter 6

Spoils

Having slept most of the day away, they shared a large meal and set out again late in the afternoon. Right now it was night and they were traveling through the woods. There was no moon, and it was extremely dark. Alice and Gronk, being monsters, could see perfectly well. Waldo found himself stumbling along trying to keep up.

"You are such a liar," Gronk said in his high pitched, lisping voice.

"I swear to you it's true," Alice told him.

"I can't believe it."

"It happened."

"Is it so, master?" Gronk looked back over his shoulder. "Did you really get thrown into a river?"

"Why are you telling him about this?" Waldo demanded. "It's not as though it matters."

"I just thought he ought to know the sort of trouble you get yourself into," Alice said. "So he can be ready the next time it happens."

"When have I ever gotten into trouble?"

In the dark he thought he saw her raise an eyebrow. Through their bond he clearly felt her disbelief. "Do you really want me to answer darling?"

"No, probably not."

"So you really did get tossed into a river?"

Waldo tried to wave the question away. "I was caught off guard."

"Exactly how do you get surprised by an angry mob?" As he was walking along, Gronk casually reached down and ripped a bush out of the ground, roots and all. He tore off a branch and began eating it.

Alice gawked at him. "Are you still hungry? You ate four whole fish and eight squirrels. And you ate them raw!"

Grinning, he patted his belly. "I'm an ogre. I'm always hungry. It's all right. I can eat most anything." He shoved another chunk of shrub into his mouth.

"I've noticed." Having seen him eat an entire squirrel in a gulp, Alice had no doubts at all about the stories she'd heard. It was said ogres ate everything they killed, whether it be animal, human, or monster.

"As long as you don't ever try to eat us," Alice told him.

"Oh, don't worry, I would never do that. Not unless I was really, really, really hungry." Gronk crammed the rest of the bush into his mouth. The sound of it crunching and snapping was quite audible.

"I think we should bring extra food with us from now on," Waldo said.

Alice nodded her agreement.

XXX

Stumbling blindly through the woods, Waldo was forced to take hold of Alice's hand to keep from getting completely lost. He could have cast a fire spell to light his way, but any flame would have made him a target for anything sitting out in the dark.

He tripped on some unseen rock or chunk of earth and nearly fell. Alice had to grab him to keep him upright. "Do you want to stop for a bit, dear?"

"I'm fine," he assured her as he tried to get his bearings. He was not good at telling directions in the best of times. In near total darkness, he had no idea where they were headed. "Are you sure this way is north?"

"Yes."

"How can you tell?"

"Because the sun sets in the west, you can figure which way is north. This was north when the sun was still up, so it will be now."

"So really, we could be going in circles?"

"Do you want to stop until morning?"

Waldo considered it. His instinct was to try and cover as much ground as possible until they reached Norwich. He had no doubt his grandfather pursued them. On the other hand, he felt as though they were trying to navigate a maze while blindfolded. Having to hold Alice's hand the entire time did not help. He was supposed to be the one in control of the situation. Being led about like a child really wasn't the image he wanted. "Perhaps we could stop for a short time and see if the stars and moon come out."

Not too far away, Waldo could hear the snapping of a tree branch, followed by the sound of aggressive chewing. "Want to stop and ask for directions, master?"

"From whom?"

"There's a camp fire up ahead," Gronk said between bites.

Surprised, Waldo scanned the darkness. Sure enough, he spotted a glimmer slipping through a thick copse of trees.

"They must have dug a pit and banked the fire," Alice said. "It's not giving off much light."

"Who do you suppose they are?" Waldo asked.

"A patrol of soldiers. We're getting near the marshes where the goblins live. There are always patrols out looking for any who decide to go raiding."

Waldo tapped his chin. "Then let's meet with them. They can tell us if we are headed north and how far we are from Norwich."

"Uh, darling? That might not be such a good idea. The patrols attack monsters on sight. What happens when they see an ogre?"

"I am sure being owned by a White Mage will make it all right." Waldo began to carefully make his way toward the light. "Gronk, stay behind me until I explain things."

"Yes, master."

Alice let out a sigh and walked beside him.

XXX

Certain the soldiers would show the proper respect to someone in white robes, Waldo stepped directly into the clearing. "Greeting. I am Waldo Rabbit, and I…"

He stopped talking when he got a clear view of the camp.

As Alice suspected, there was a fire pit with dirt piled up around its edge. There were five children, three boys and two girls, their ages ranging from six to ten. Four of them were tied about a tree trunk, their mouths gagged. The fifth child, a pudgy boy, was bound hand and foot to a wooden pole. A pair of goblins were getting ready to put him over the flames to begin roasting.

The two creatures turned their malformed heads and stared at him, tiny coal black eyes glistened in the firelight. They wore dirty leather jerkins and bits and pieces of armor about their arms and legs. They seemed as startled as Waldo.

Then one of the goblins dropped his end of the pole and screeched. "Magi! Kill! Kill!" From the ground he, snatched up a heavy two sided axe.

The other one let go of the pole as well, and grabbed a broadsword from a sheath on its back. Both of them stomped forward as fast as their stubby legs could carry them.

To Waldo's right came the sound of muscle tearing as Alice transformed. The goblin with the axe gave a startled, "Gra?" It did not hesitate, though, as it tried to cleave Alice in two.

Compared to humans, goblins are very strong, but they are not agile or fast.

Alice darted back to let the axe slice through the air in front of her and then dashed forward before the homely beast could bring it back around. Her right hand was a blur. Before the goblin even knew it, blood was gushing out from its throat. The dying monster dropped its weapon, stumbled back, and fell.

Waldo only saw this on the periphery as the second creature was coming at him. He drew his wand and used it. "*Pyro!*" He sent out a stream of fire right into the belly of his target.

The flames caught and spread, like with a piece of fat thrown into a cook fire. The goblin was completely alight, yet it kept running towards him, the sword held high.

"Grrrrrooooooooooooooooooo!" the monster wailed even as Waldo kept pouring fire into it.

The goblin was just about to reach him, when his ogre suddenly jumped out of the woods. The sword came down with enough force to cut a man clean in two, but the blade simply bounced off of the ogre's thick hide.

"Gronk smash!" he roared without any hint of lisp. He brought a fist down on the goblin's turnip shaped head. It exploded, much like a pumpkin being struck by a mallet: skin, bone, blood, and gray goo splattered. The rest of the body, still burning, shuddered and fell. The short fight was over.

XXX

"Are you all right, darling?"

"I am fine, thanks to you and Gronk." Alice had saved his life before. Now Gronk had as well, Waldo nodded to his second familiar. "Thank you, Gronk." Dark Mages were not supposed to say, "thank you." He had been taught thanking others was beneath him and a sign of weakness. It was one more of the new things he had learned to do since setting out.

The ogre had a wide, tusked smile and gave him a wink. "Gronk happy save master. Maybe master punish Gronk later?"

"That seems fair."

Alice gave a sour grunt and muttered something about "weird stuff" beneath her breath. She then began to walk towards the tree where the children were bound. "Are you dears all right? I'll take care of you."

As if on cue, they all began to desperately try to wriggle out of the ropes. Waldo could clearly hear muffled screams coming through their gags.

"It's fine." Alice held her hands out reassuringly. "The goblins are dead. There is nothing to be scared of anymore."

"You mean except for the succubus with wings, claws, horns, fangs, and tail who just happens to be covered in goblin blood?" Waldo pointed out. "They might be terrified of seeing an ogre, as well."

"Gronk no know why." He casually reached down to the corpse at his feet and tore an arm off at the shoulder. Schunk! "Gronk no scary." He took a mouthful and chewed it before swallowing it down. "Cook goblin more good than raw. Master want?"

"Maybe later."

There were more muffled screams.

Alice quickly transformed back to her human self. Her hands, while no longer clawed, were still drenched in wet blood, as was most of her front. Grabbing a cloth rag from one of the corpses, she quickly wiped off as much as she could while trying to calm the children. "It's all right. You're safe now. No one is going to hurt you." She turned to her husband. "Isn't that so, darling?"

"Of course." Waldo nodded. He spoke directly to the children. "I promise none of you will be harmed."

"See? You are all safe."

"As my new slaves, you will be fed and treated fairly so long as you obey me."

"What?" Alice asked in disbelief.

"If you defy me, I will feed you to the ogre."

High pitched, muffled screams continued from their little throats.

Alice waved her hands. "He is joking! He doesn't mean it!"

"Yes, I do."

"No, you don't," Alice growled.

"Can Gronk eat fat one?"

The boy tied to the pole cried and tried his awkward best to roll away.

"You are not eating any of the children!" Alice told him.

"No eat all, just skin, fat ones always taste more good."

"Don't eat the slaves, Gronk," Waldo said. "At least not until they do something to deserve it."

Alice stared at him. "I don't believe you."

"What? You want me to make an example of one now?"

She stomped to him and spoke in a whisper reminding him of steel being sharpened. "You are not making slaves of these poor children."

Waldo paused and considered. "Well, I suppose I could sell them instead. Kids aren't worth as much as healthy adults, but I'm sure they'll fetch a decent price. Especially the girls. There is always a demand for little girls. Do you know if there is a slave market in Norwich?"

"We don't have slaves in this country."

"I bought you, remember?"

"I wasn't a slave. I was an indentured servant."

"I don't care what they call it so long as I get a reasonable price."

"These children don't belong to you!"

"Yes, they do," Waldo insisted. "It's called spoils of battle. When you destroy an enemy, you collect everything of value they possess. There is nothing wrong with taking spoils. I mean, are we not going to take their weapons and anything else we find?"

"Swords don't have parents."

"Do you mean I can keep the ones who are orphans?"

Alice glared at him.

"You're serious about this."

"In Cannassa's name, of course I am!"

"If I don't claim them, what am I supposed to do instead?"

"We take them to their families."

Waldo quirked an eyebrow. "How does returning them help me with my quest?"

"It's the right thing to do."

Waldo sighed. "You know, Alice, you have far too many ridiculous morals and rules, and they're always inconvenient. Don't Charm... don't steal from people unless they try to have their way with you... don't torture as a reward... pay for things... don't turn children into slaves. You really need to be more reasonable."

Alice crossed her arms over her chest. "We are taking them home."

He knew how stubborn she could be when it came to these silly rules of hers. "Fine, but I want something from you in return."

Her cheeks blushed, and through their bond he could sense eagerness.

"You want to have your way with me again?"

"Well, yes, but we both know that will happen soon enough regardless." Her face turned a couple shades brighter. "What I want is for you to agree to Charm someone when I ask."

"If we take the kids back to their folks I will do it once."

"I am giving up five slaves. Shouldn't that be worth at least five Charms?"

Alice frowned but nodded. "Deal."

Chapter 7

Doing the Right Thing

When Alice cut the ropes and freed the children, their immediate reaction was to make a run for it. She was forced to chase after them and return them to the camp. Fortunately, she could see through the dark while the kids could not, so it wasn't too difficult. When they realized they couldn't run away, the five children huddled together and wailed that they were all going to be eaten.

Despite Alice's best efforts, she couldn't calm them. Eventually, she asked Waldo to tell them they would be all right.

Waldo told the children they would be safe, as long as they stopped crying and annoying him.

Oddly enough, this actually worked, and the children quieted.

As Alice got them some food and Gronk continued to eat the goblins, Waldo searched the camp for anything worth taking. There were no coins, but the creatures appeared to have grab anything made of metal. He soon discovered a cast iron pot and pan, four daggers, the head of a shovel, nine rusty nails, and bits and pieces of armor including two sets of badly mangled chain mail and a dented iron helmet. Added to this were the axe and sword the goblins had used. It was not exactly an impressive haul, but they would take everything.

Once the spoils were gathered and everyone was done eating, Waldo wanted to get going. He wished to return the kids as quickly as possible.

The children, though, had no idea what direction to travel in the dark. Alice convinced him it would be best to make camp for the night and take them back come the morning. Waldo was not pleased but agreed.

XXX

The Following Morning, Gronk was sitting in the grass as Waldo took care of him.

"Feel good, Master."

"I am glad you think so, Gronk."

"Where Master learn do this?"

"My mother taught me, one of the many skills she felt it necessary for me to learn."

"Master's hands feel soooooooooo good on Gronk's skin. Gronk like."

"Well, my mother forced me to practice on dozens of slaves until I had the technique down."

As Waldo worked on taking care of his ogre, Alice stood about ten feet away looking on. Her right foot was tapping away as one hand kept tugging at some of her hair.

"Why are you doing this where the children can see?" She waved at the kids who were all staring wide eyed.

"Why would I care?"

"They're going to get the wrong idea," Alice said.

"What? How I'm a master who takes care of his servants? If anything, I think it a fine lesson."

She began tugging at her hair more violently. "It looks weird... unnatural even."

"I am just providing Gronk with what he needs." Waldo's fingers continued moving relentlessly across the ogre's pea green skin. "I didn't hear any complaints when I took care of myself or you this morning."

"That was different. We're married, so it's okay for us to do those sorts of things. Anyway, we were inside the tent where no one could see."

Gronk sent her a tusked smile. "Gronk no fit in tent. Alice like better if Master and Gronk go out in wood where nobody see?"

Alice quickly shook her head.

"You're going to need to get used to this, Alice." Waldo told her. "It's going to be a daily routine. From now on I'll be doing this every morning."

"Really, darling?"

Waldo nodded. "It's necessary. If I don't take care of this, bad things could happen. Anyway I am about done."

He drew the last of the protective runes over Gronk's back, writing them in ashes with his fingertips.

"*Loratos est videtur.*" He cast a spell sending a little of his magical energy into the runes. The ash faded from sight as the wards were activated and hidden. "There, now all three of us are shielded from magical detection and guarded against magical attack. We can finally get going."

"I still say it looks weird," Alice muttered.

XXX

As they were tramping through the woods, the kids all concentrated around Waldo. It was to be expected they would want to stay as far away from Gronk as possible. While Alice was in her human form once more and trying her best to coax the children into walking with her, they all remembered her with claws and horns. Being the only one the children had not seen turn into a monster, they apparently felt Waldo to be the safest alternative, the previous night's talk about enslavement and possibly being fed to the ogre notwithstanding.

Waldo merely accepted it was his curse to be the loveable one.

XXX

Waldo was thinking about what had happened last night. Despite being taken by surprise, he had not hesitated to draw his wand and fight. As with the encounter with his grandfather he'd been ready and willing to use lethal magic. By all rights, yesterday should have had his first kill. Who knew goblins took so long to cook?

Even though Gronk had needed to intervene and do the actual killing, Waldo was feeling rather proud of himself. Clearly, since setting out on his quest, he had gotten stronger. He had survived an attack from an angry mob, robbed a hedgewizard, escaped an archlich, outsmarted a White Mage, and acquired two Great Monsters as his familiars. He was pretty amazing.

Waldo could see he was becoming harder. Facing dangers out in the real world was definitely making him a true Dark Mage. All the weaknesses were being worn away. Soon only his true self would remain, a man without remorse or pity who cared only about himself. A merciless, black hearted fiend capable of any sort of cruelty or perversion. A terrifying...

He felt a tug on his robes and looked down. One of the boys was looking up at him. "Yes?"

"Lord Rabbit, thank you for making my rash go away."

Waldo waved it off. "It was nothing. I wanted to practice a little of my healing magic. And the proper title when addressing a mage is 'Master' not 'Lord or 'Sir.'"

The boy nodded with a goofy grin on his face.

Waldo looked away and tried to get back to his thoughts. A terrifying and unpredictable force. All who looked upon him would quiver in... He was again interrupted by someone yanking on his robes. It was the fat boy who had been tied to the pole. "Yes?"

"Thank you for saving me. Not only from the goblins but from the ogre too, I was really scared I was going to be eaten."

"Then may want to go on a diet. It helps to be able to run and to not look like the main course of a meal."

The boy's eyes widened, and his head wobbled up and down.

Waldo refocused. All who looked upon him would quiver with fear. For he would be the cruelest, wickedest, and most dreaded Dark Mage in all the land!

"Master Rabbit?"

Waldo looked down. There was an eight-year-old girl with messy chestnut hair and eyes the color of mud staring up excitedly. He thought her name was Jenna. "Yes?"

She held her hands up and waved them about excitedly. "Again!"

Waldo sighed and pulled out his wand. "Fine, but this is the last time. *Levitarus.*"

The girl lifted ten feet into the air and gave a squeal of pure delight. She began flopping her arms and legs about as if she could control where she went. Waldo motioned his wand to move her slowly through the air in front of him. Jenna was laughing and wriggling, having the time of her life.

As this was happening, Waldo heard a loud snort from behind him. He turned to see Gronk's grin. Through their bond, Waldo could sense amusement.

"What? She kept bothering me about using my magic to make her fly. Since Alice won't let me gag her, this is the only way to get her to stop."

Gronk nodded, though the smirk didn't change at all. "Gronk see Master know what he do."

Waldo then shifted his gaze to Alice. Through their connection, he perceived she was also pleased. Though her emotions were more... maternal?

"What?"

She brought her hands together and sighed. "You're going to make a wonderful father someday."

"Huh?"

Meanwhile, Jenna began shouting for him to send her higher into the air.

XXX

They finally stumbled across the village where the children came from. It was a little place called Peabody and looked like every other small village in this part of Lothas.

There had been a huge commotion among the villagers as the children were quickly reunited with their parents. A big bearded fellow by the name of Lorimer addressed them. "Thank you,

Master Rabbit, for returning our little ones to us." The man performed an awkward bow, and most of the villagers followed his example. "We are truly grateful to you."

"You have an odd way of showing it."

Every man except for Lorimer was armed with either a spear, a rusty sword, or a bow. The archers had them nocked and drawn.

"Ah, please forgive us for being wary. It is not you we fear." Lorimer's eyes went past him and settled on Gronk. "We suffered an ogre attack recently. An entire family was slaughtered and eaten."

Gronk planted his hands on his hips. "Maybe they asking for it, you no know. Humans no think about ogre side."

This made all the men grip their weapons a little tighter and caused the mothers to hold their children close to them.

Alice tried to elbow Gronk in the ribs but wasn't quite tall enough to manage. She got him around the hips instead.

"I confess I am more than a little surprised to see a White Mage traveling with such a beast. Another White Mage came here and killed the one that attacked us. She made it very clear her order didn't believe monsters should be allowed to live."

"She really said that?" Alice asked, looking rather unhappy.

"She did. Doesn't Master Rabbit feel the same?"

"Well, of course I do. I am a White Mage, after all," Waldo gave his robes a shake as if to draw extra attention to them. "I prefer to work them to death, is all."

"Ah, as you say, Master Rabbit."

One of the boys who'd been returned picked this moment to point at Alice and shout. "She's a monster, too! I saw her with horns and claws and wings! She was gonna eat us, but Master Rabbit stopped her!" His mother quieted him, but the other children all nodded.

"The kids went through a lot," Waldo said. "Obviously they're a bit confused."

"It's not surprising."

"Master Rabbit wanted to make us slaves," one of the girls said. Her mother immediately smacked her on top of the head and told her to be silent.

"Anyway, this other White Mage, her name wouldn't have been Melissa by any chance, would it?"

"Why, yes, do you know Mistress Cornwall?"

"As a matter of fact, we ran into each other in Middleton a few days ago. She did me a great favor."

"Ah, well, good. Hopefully, you will meet her again soon."

"With my luck, I probably will. I am going to Norwich, could you tell me how to get there?"

"Norwich is about three days travel to the northeast. If you follow the path outside our gate, it will take you to the main road five miles from here."

Waldo nodded. "Sounds simple enough."

Lorimer glanced to Gronk and back. "You won't be allowed to take your ogre into Norwich. They don't permit monsters."

"Really? I know Stratford allows them, and Middleton has hundreds if not thousands of them."

"That may be, but they're not by the marshlands. They don't have to deal with raiders. I expect your ogre will be killed on sight, even if he is travelling with you."

"I see. Well, good to know."

This was not happy news. Norwich was where he was supposed to find his third familiar. How could there be a Great Monster living in a city where monsters were forbidden? Normally, Waldo would assume Enver lied to him. However, he had found Alice and Gronk where Enver's map said they would be. It only seemed logical to assume the third monster would be there, too.

Well, he would go and search regardless. It was not as if he had a better option.

As Waldo was thinking, Alice noted a wooden pole in the center on the village common with ten long strips of colored ribbon running down from the top of it. "Oh, you have a summer's pole ready. Is it almost the summer solstice?"

"It's tomorrow," Lorimer said. "We would invite you to stay and join us, but I am sure Master Rabbit wants to waste no time getting to Norwich."

"The solstice is tomorrow?" Waldo asked. "It completely slipped my mind."

"Could we stay and celebrate it?" Alice asked.

Waldo immediately shook his head. "There is no time to waste, but I promise we will do something on the road."

"Great," Alice sighed.

"The village would normally want to give you some sort of reward for what you've done," Lorimer said. "But I know White Mages don't believe in such things."

"Yes, we do," Waldo said.

Lorimer looked at him in surprise. "Mistress Cornwall said her order didn't fight for rewards. The only thing she asked was for us to remember her service and tell others about it."

"Obviously, Melissa is an idiot. I'll take as much as you want to give me."

Alice quickly strode to Waldo's side, waving her hands. "My husband is joking, of course we don't want anything. Knowing these children are safe again is reward enough."

"No, it's not."

Alice turned to him with a rigid smile and grabbed his elbow hard enough to make him flinch. "Yes, it is."

He really did hate her silly rules. "Right, I am joking. I do that some times. Because who would want to get a reward they can actually spend when they can get nothing instead?"

Lorimer blinked and turned to the red haired woman. "Another joke?"

"Of course," Alice said as she poked Waldo in the ribs. "My husband never knows when to stop."

"Well, we do sincerely thank you and promise to tell everyone about the heroic Waldo Rabbit." Lorimer bowed once more as did everyone else.

"Wonderful." Rubbing his side, Waldo turned to go. "Oh, and Unity, Justice, and Peace and all that."

XXX

As Jenna's mother was taking her home, the girl spoke: "Momma?"

"Yes?"

"Master Rabbit says the White Mages are plotting to take over the world."

"That's nice, honey."

Chapter 8

An Alterothan Tradition

They eventually found the main road and were finally on the way to Norwich again. As they went, they crossed paths with other travelers a few times. On each occasion, the folk would get one look at Gronk and either scramble off the road or turn and flee in the opposite direction. Apparently, the people in this part of Lothas were too terrified to get anywhere near an ogre, even when accompanied by a White Mage. It was obvious to Waldo he would need to do something about the situation before they arrived at the city.

As they walked, he pulled out his wand as well as one of his knives and began to do a little carving.

XXX

The horrible ball of fire began to sink toward the horizon. Waldo led them off of the road and into the forest. He found a small clearing surrounded by thick scrub brush and trees with low branches.

"This place should do." He turned to Gronk. "Dig me a fire pit about four feet deep, five feet across, and bank the dirt around its edge, so it won't give off too much light. Alice, I want you to gather firewood, enough for a bonfire."

"Whatever you say, Master." With the children gone, Gronk was back to using his high pitched, lisping voice again. Not bothering with any tools, the ogre began ripping up grass and dirt with his massive hands.

Alice didn't immediately move to obey. Instead she put both hands on her hips and raised an eyebrow. "What are you doing?"

"Well, obviously I want to build a bonfire, but without having people for miles able to see it."

"Yes, I understand that part, but why?"

"Today is the solstice and I want the three of us to celebrate it."

"Huh, that's nice I suppose, though it would have been better if we could have stayed in the village."

"It will be simpler this way. In any case, you and Gronk should both be grateful I am willing to allow you to join me."

Alice chuckled and rolled her eyes. "Of course, darling." She wandered off to start gathering firewood. As Alice and Gronk worked Waldo built a small separate campfire. He filled the cook pot with water. Waldo then reached into one of the many pockets of his robes for a cloth sack. Opening it, Waldo dumped the contents onto his hand: three stubby grey mushrooms with thick stalks and slightly wrinkled caps with black spots.

Wolfsbane mushrooms.

He brought them to his nose and took a quick sniff. There was a strong, distinctive scent reminding him of a mix between mildew and a piece of meat gone bad. The mushrooms had gotten their name because wolves would sometimes eat them. The creatures would then become insanely violent, lashing out and attacking anything near shortly before going into convulsions and dying as blood poured from their mouth and anus.

Waldo casually tossed the mushrooms into the pot and set it atop the fire.

XXX

By the time the fire pit was dug and Alice had brought in enough armfuls of wood, the horrible ball of fire had gone from the sky. The stars were shining along with a sliver of the moon. Waldo stood by the edge of the pit with his wand.

"*Pyro.*" A steady stream of fire poured from the tip of his wand and washed over the pieces of wood. In no time, there was a roaring blaze filling the clearing with light and heat.

Nodding, he put his wand away and went back to the pot. The water had been boiling for well over an hour. With great care, he poured the water out, dousing the campfire. The mushrooms had puffed up some and become soft to the touch. Waldo spread a piece of cloth on the grass and speared each mushroom with a knife before placing it down. Choosing the most tender, Waldo sliced off the stalk and cut the cap in half. Then, holding one of the halves between thumb and forefinger, he very slowly and very carefully cut off two slivers that were as thin as parchment. "These should do."

"Ah, darling?" Alice had been standing nearby watching. "Do we start dancing and singing around the fire now?"

"In a bit. First we need to get ready." Standing, he undid his robe and let it fall to the ground. Waldo then unbuttoned his shirt.

"What are you doing?"

"Preparing to celebrate the Solstice," Waldo tossed aside his shirt, trousers and shoes. "Well what are you waiting for? You and Gronk get naked, too."

"What?" Alice choked out.

"Oooh, now this is the kind of party I like." Gronk needed no further encouragement. His burlap loincloth was quickly gone, and he stood in all of his green skinned glory.

Alice's eyes boggled when she got a clear look at what was hanging between Gronk's thighs. The size and dimensions reminded her of a club carved from green wood. She swiftly turned her head to stare at her husband. By this time, all his clothes were off, and he was standing in front of her. She had seen his body plenty of times now, but it had always been in private.

"Well? What are you waiting for Alice?" Waldo asked.

"Why are you naked?!"

"I already told you," Waldo impatiently reminded her. "I want to celebrate the summer solstice."

"What does that have to do with taking our clothes off? People feast and dance with all of their clothes on."

"I don't care about whatever barbaric customs people follow here. We are going to celebrate the holiday in accordance with my traditions. Admittedly, this is less than ideal. There should be ginger cakes and slaves to oil us and play drums." Waldo shrugged. "We will have to make the best of it."

"I am not undressing in front of Gronk."

"Oh, don't worry about me. Sweetie. It's not you I'll be looking at." The ogre sent a big smile Waldo's way.

"That doesn't make me feel better!"

"Alice, are you saying you're not going to respect my culture?"

"Not when it involves me being naked in public."

"There are only the three of us."

"It's still one too many."

"Don't worry, Master. If she wants to sit out. it's fine by me. I don't mind if it's only us two."

"I thank you, Gronk. I am glad at least one of you appreciates my efforts to include you in this celebration." Waldo turned to the only person still wearing clothes. "Really, Alice? I expected better from you."

"Hey! What's with the tone? Most husbands would think their wives refusing to undress in front of others a good thing."

"These would be the same men who would want to have you burned at the stake for being a succubus?"

"I never said they were perfect."

"Alice, I don't see what the problem is here. I just want to celebrate the solstice like I always have and would like you and Gronk to join me. I thought you would be pleased. I mean, look how happy Gronk is."

"I'm so joyful I may burst into song."

"You see?"

One look in his direction told Alice he was both happy *and* excited.

"Fine!" she snapped and yanked her blouse open. "But I'm only doing it to make sure something tragic doesn't happen." Alice soon had all her clothes off and neatly folded on the ground. She pressed her knees together and kept her arms crossed over her ample chest. She didn't really mind Waldo seeing her like this. Anyway, not too much. It was Gronk's presence that bothered her.

"Nice ass," the ogre lisped. "Mine is still cuter, though."

"Shut. Your. Mouth."

"Here." Waldo handed her one of the thin slices of mushroom. "Chew it and swallow."

She held it between thumb and forefinger. "Darling, are you sure about this? Everyone knows wolfsbane mushrooms are lethal."

"Pretty sure." He popped his portion into his mouth and munched.

She shook her head. "At least poisoning each other is a romantic way to die." She bit down. "Auuggh! It tastes like rotten cabbage!"

Waldo swallowed his. "You don't eat it for the taste. Here, Gronk," he held out the remaining mushrooms. "Even for an ogre, this much should effect you."

"Thanks, Master." Gronk ate them without complaint.

Alice made a face but got it down. "What happens now?

"We dance around the fire howling until the wolfsbane takes effect, and we fall asleep. It will give us all the most vivid dreams about what we either want or fear most."

"Seriously?"

Waldo nodded. "It would be better if our skins were oiled down and there were drums… but still…" He put his head back. "Ahhhhoooooo!!!!" Waldo shook his hands in the air and stomped about the bonfire.

"Woo hoo! Let the wild things out!" Gronk followed his master's lead, jumping around and shaking his hips fervently.

"This is so embarrassing." Alice halfheartedly walked about the fire as Waldo and Gronk kept shouting and gyrating.

Before long, the wolfsbane began to do its work. First Waldo, then Alice, and finally Gronk fell unconscious.

They dreamed.

XXX

Gronk found himself in a dungeon.

He was naked and bound face down to a massive iron rack. Thick chains and manacles held his wrists and ankles in place. He tried pulling free, only to find he was trapped and helpless.

"Now, Gronk, I will teach you what happens to those who defy me."

Gronk twisted his head to look over his shoulder. Standing behind him was his master. Waldo was all grown up, though, his blond hair cut short, and many scars raked across the left side of his face. Master was bare chested, his skin glistening in the torchlight. All he wore was a pair of skin tight leather trousers. In his right hand was a six-foot long whip.

"I think we'll start with the Trapped Bear and then move onto the Lonely Shepard Boy."

Master brought his hand back and delivered an expert strike to Gronk's bare backside. It made the ogre feel all tingly and excited. "Yes! Punish me, Master! I've been a bad, bad ogre!"

XXX

Alice found herself in a large room. There was an arching ceiling twenty feet above, the walls were all of gray stone. A thick, luxuriant brown carpet covered the floor. A pair of open balconies looked upon a rich green land. Instinctively, she knew she was in a castle, and it had to be her husband's.

Laughter rang as six small children surrounded her, running about at play. Three boys and three girls, all of them with yellow hair and yellow eyes, perfect matches for Waldo's. They were pink and plump and happy.

A sense of warmth filled her heart, and Alice found herself smiling from ear to ear. This was what she had always wanted, a happy, loving home with a dear husband and precious children. What could be better?

One of the little girls suddenly stopped and looked in her direction.

"Momma!" she squealed and took off running.

"Oh, come here, honey," Alice bent and held her arms out. The girl ran past her. "Wait, honey, where are you…" Alice stood and turned about to see another woman in the room behind her.

It was Melissa, the one Waldo had met in the bar, dressed in a silk gown of white so pure it hurt the eyes to look at it. On the top of her head was a thin circlet of gold. The woman looked regal, like a princess from an old tale. Melissa snatched the little girl and held her aloft as she laughed and kicked her feet.

The other children all rushed past, so they, too, could crowd around Melissa. Each of them called out to gain her attention. Little hands were held up in hopes they too might be picked up, as well.

"What are you doing here?" Alice demanded.

Melissa glanced at her dismissively. "Where else should a mother be but with her children?"

"They're not your children. They're mine!"

Melissa set the little girl back down. "Your attitude makes you a good nanny, but you need to watch your tongue."

"Nanny?" Alice choked on the word.

Waldo strolled into the room. Unlike Melissa, he was dressed in the same black robes as when she'd first met him. On his head, though, was a slightly thicker gold circlet.

"Greetings, my love." He placed a light kiss on Melissa's lips. Then, he beamed at the little ones. "How are my beautiful children?"

In answer there was a chorus of, "Poppa."

Alice shook her head. "Darling! What is going on here?"

"What do you mean?"

"Why are you kissing that woman, and why is she pretending to be the mother of your children?"

Waldo quirked an eyebrow. "Because she is my beloved wife and the mother of my children."

"I am your wife! She must have you under some sort of spell!"

"Oh, not this again." Melissa sighed and turned to Waldo. "You were the one who insisted we keep her."

He shrugged. "She's good with kids. Alice, we were married, but that was a long time ago, before I fell in love with Melissa and returned home. Now she is my wife, and you are the nanny."

"But you love me!"

"Where did you get such an idea? I never actually said it, did I? And you must know a man sleeping with a woman doesn't mean he loves her. It simply means he is a man. The way you were constantly forcing yourself on me, it's not as if I had much choice."

"But…"

Melissa wrapped herself around his arm and placed her head on his shoulder. "It is only natural for the two of us to be together. We are both mages who were traveling the world. Of course I can understand him in ways you couldn't possibly. I mean, even our hair and eyes match. We're perfect for each other. Why would he ever want some silly barmaid who is not even human?"

"You wanted to kill him!"

"So? What wife doesn't want to kill her husband from time to time?"

"Aren't you still a White Mage? Doesn't that make you his mortal enemy?"

"You're describing most marriages."

"Plus," Waldo added. "Your breasts are starting to sag."

"Erk!" She covered her chest with both arms.

The youngest child, a girl of perhaps two, tugged at Melissa's skirt.

"What is it, dear?"

"Wanda make poo."

"Your nanny will take care of it. What else is she here for?" Melisa then smiled at Waldo. "Want to make savage, violent, love to me right here in front of the children?"

"Sure." He pushed her down onto the carpet as the children formed a circle and danced about them singing.

"But… they… you…" Alice couldn't form a sentence as she watched him yanking off Melissa's dress.

Meanwhile, the two-year-old pulled on her hand. "Poo poo, nanny, poo poo."

The little girl led Alice out of the room.

In a daze Alice looked back over her shoulder. "My breasts are not saggy!"

Little Wanda looked up and gave a shake of her head.

XXX

Waldo found himself alone in the middle of the woods.

Alice and Gronk were both nowhere to be seen, and even the bonfire was gone. It was only him beneath a night sky.

"Disappointing," he sighed. Waldo then noticed he was wearing his old robes again. "Well, that's something at least, though I would have liked to have gone back to the castle."

A girlish laugh drifted from the forest.

He immediately had his wand in hand. Waldo noted it was his current one, the one made of soulwood. Old robes and new wand; it was an intriguing combination.

Stepping out of the woods was a figure in black robes with a lowered hood. For an instant, Waldo thought it was his mother. The form was clearly feminine, with raven hair and pale skin, but the curves were not quite voluptuous enough to be his mother's.

"If you are disappointed, you have only yourself to blame, little brother. This is your own mind, after all." He recognized the voice. It was Gwendolyn's. But it was not the rasp of the sister trapped in a mirror. It was the soft, lyrical voice she'd had when she was still flesh and blood.

He lowered his wand. "Gwen, is that you?"

She approached without hesitation. "It's me, little brother."

As she came to stand before him, he was able to get a clear look. It was her. Not the ghost from the mirror, but the girl he had grown up with. She appeared to be sixteen and as alive and well as she'd been on the morning she set out on her First Quest. Her throat was still whole, and her cheeks were rosy. There was even that old teasing glint in her brown eyes.

She held out her arms.

Waldo immediately rushed forward to embrace her. He squeezed tight. Her arms wrapped around him, as well. Waldo shut his eyes and welcomed the warmth and feel of her as they hugged. It had been such a long time.

"I've missed you." He was embarrassed to hear his voice straining. He was not going to cry like some child.

"I know," she said. He could feel one hand gently patting the back of his head. "You've gotten big. The last time we did this, you were twelve."

He knew this was an illusion, a dream. When you ate the wolfsbane, the hallucinations were always incredibly vivid. Knowing that didn't make it feel any less real. For this short time, Gwen was with him again. He embraced her for long minutes. Waldo didn't want to say anything. He only wanted to hold her for as long as he could.

Gwendolyn seemed quite content to let him. She returned his hug in silence, one hand rubbing the back of his head, as if he were a child again.

Eventually he did let go. He quickly rubbed his eyes to get rid of any moisture.

Smiling, she stretched her arms up over her head. "It's so nice not being trapped in the mirror for a change. Stepping into the world, even if it's a false one, is so much better than being, a mere observer."

"Wait, are you really Gwen or my imagination?"

"Yes."

The look on his face must have been amusing because she laughed. "You're going to tell me that I have to let you have your fun since you're dead."

She nodded. "You know me well, little brother."

"This must be a delusion. You can't be the real Gwen."

"Why not? You know the stories about spirits contacting people in their dreams. We were always very close. It would only make sense if I were able to appear to you."

"You never have before."

She shrugged. "Your mind is especially open right now, and you felt a strong urge to see me. Those circumstances might have made a difference."

He considered her words. It was possible. Maybe this really was the spirit of his sister manifested within his dream.

"Or maybe I am nothing more than your imagination. I could be one or the other."

"Couldn't you tell me?"

She had an amused grin. "No."

"Ruin your fun?"

"Perhaps, and whatever I tell you, you can't really prove one way or the other. At least not while you are still dreaming." She craned her neck to look up above. "You know, I'd forgotten how beautiful the stars are."

"I don't like them. They're unnatural. The skies should be perfectly black at night."

"You only think so because you grew up in Alter. To the rest of the world, this is natural. In many, many ways our home is the exception to what is viewed as 'normal.' Haven't you realized this yet?"

"What I have come to realize is Alteroth is the only civilized place on Earth."

"Everyone thinks the same little brother, no matter where you travel, people always think their way is the right one."

"The only difference is I happen to be right."

She laughed, though Waldo was not sure why.

Gwendolyn glanced back up at the night sky. "This reminds me of being on my quest. Did you know those moments were the best of my life?"

"You're joking."

"Hardly."

"You left Alteroth, traveled through the Barrens, walked for hundreds of miles across a desert surrounded by strangers. You must have suffered. How can you say those were your best moments?"

"It's because for the first and only time in my life I was free, little brother. I was happy enough living in the castle with you and everyone else. I loved mother, and she loved me, in her tyrannical and horribly brutal way."

Waldo nodded, understanding perfectly.

"When I left on my First Quest, I was suddenly free. I realized I could do anything I wanted without needing to worry about what mother would think. The entire world was open to me, and everything seemed possible. It was such a glorious adventure."

"But you died! You had your throat slit."

"I remember the first night I spent outside of Alteroth." There was a wistful longing in her voice. "I camped on the top of a hill overlooking a valley. The ground was covered in jasmine. I ate a suckling pig I'd killed with my own two hands. All around me the flowers bloomed, and I fell asleep with their sweet scent filling the air under the stars. Even now, I can shut my eyes and smell the blossoms. The memory is a happy one for me, and what happened later doesn't change it."

"I always thought you were miserable, off in some forsaken land far from home."

"I won't lie. Walking for miles through a desert wearing black robes wasn't exactly pleasant, but there is always good mixed with the bad. Haven't you enjoyed your travels so far?"

"Which part? Almost drowning, fighting for my life against Grandfather, or having to trick a White Mage who wanted to execute me?"

"So none of it has been any fun at all?"

"Well… I did like losing my virginity."

"I'll bet."

"And, I suppose, my time with Alice hasn't been all bad."

Gwen rolled her eyes and let out a giggle. "Yes, being with a succubus who is in love with you and constantly showing you affection. It must have been awful."

"Hey, it wasn't all pleasant, you know! She is always pushing me down and kissing me, her silly morals keep getting in the way, I have lost track of how many times she has nearly crushed me to death in my sleep, and we keep having sex until I'm completely exhausted and worn out!"

His sister didn't say a word. She merely grinned.

Waldo could feel his cheeks getting flushed and suddenly began looking at the grass. "Okay, I don't really mind the last part."

"It's all right, little brother. Life is meant to be lived. Enjoy these moments while you can. You will have hard times soon enough."

His eyes leapt back to her. "What do you mean?"

Gwen hesitated but did finally answer. "Master and servant... do not assume that one cannot be the other. The one who holds the leash bears it, as well."

"Huh?"

From the woods there was a rustling.

"I'm going now. I don't want to watch what comes next." She shook her head slightly. "You have some odd fears, my brother."

"Wait, you're leaving?"

"Don't worry. We'll see each other again. You know how to call me to your dreams now." She put her hood up and turned away from him.

"Gwen what did you mean? Does it have to do with Alice and Gronk or my third familiar? Are you saying they are going to control me somehow?"

She gave a slight shake of her head. "You don't expect a straight answer from me do you? There's no fun in it."

"Could you at the very least answer one question for me with a yes or no?"

"You do realize I may only be a figment of your imagination, right? I mean, you're not really standing here talking to me. Right now, you're lying on the ground naked, somewhere near a bonfire."

"If you're a dream, then everything you've said doesn't really matter. But if you truly are here, there is something I want to know."

"Fine, just this once, I won't torment you. What is your question?"

"Will I find my third familiar in Norwich?"

"No." She walked swiftly into the forest. "Goodbye, Waldo. Stay safe. At least as safe as you can." She vanished from sight.

"Wait! What do you mean no? Are you saying Enver's map was wrong? Is there no third Great Monster?" Waldo hurried after her.

As he did so, a horrible figure hopped out of the shadows. Long, twisted ears, beady little eyes, and a twitchy nose confronted him.

"Gah!" Waldo jumped back and pulled out his wand. "Stay where you are."

Ignoring his words, the horrid little creature took a brazen hop forward.

Another one appeared and then another and another. Dozens of the malevolent things came from the shadows, all of them with fluffy tails madly twitching with blood lust.

Knowing he was no match for such a monstrous horde, Waldo turned to run, only to discover there were more of them behind him. They hopped out of the forest like some swarm of locust! He was completely surrounded.

"Stay back!" He waved his wand about desperately. "I'll cook the whole lot of you!"

Their throats opened and gave a deafening, "squee." Then, as one they charged. Waldo let loose a stream of fire to set several of them alight. The rest kept coming. They leapt onto his robes, little paws clutching and grabbing as they climbed and covered him.

Then he felt the tiny teeth of these murderous, flesh eating rabbits begin to nibble.

XXX

"… not saggy, no."

Alice slowly awakened.

She could feel the sunshine bathing her. The bed was very warm, and her feet were pressing against the bedpost. A familiar form snuggled up against her.

"Alice… you… are… crush… ing… me."

Her eyes half opened to the nearly purple face of her beloved husband.

"Oh, so it was all a dream," she said as she loosened her embrace and allowed Waldo to breathe again. "I am so glad."

Her head ached, and she was thirsty. Other than that everything was fine. As the bed rose and fell, she relaxed. Things were back to normal. She could forget all about that crazy dream and return to reality. "Let's stay in bed for a little while, darling. You can play with my breasts if you want. They're as soft and firm as ever, you know."

"Bed? Alice, we're not in bed."

"Hmmm?" She wasn't completely awake yet.

"Oooh," the still sleeping ogre murmured. "Yes, Master, right there."

Waldo was the only one who was fully conscious. "Uh, Alice, what are you doing with your feet?"

"Nothing, just rubbing them against the bed post."

"What you're rubbing isn't a bed post, Alice."

It took her a moment to fully open her eyes and really take in where they were. She and Waldo were lying on top of Gronk. And the three of them were completely naked. What she was rubbing her feet against was definitely NOT a bed post.

"Aaaaaaaahhhhh!" With a blood curdling scream, she bolted off her resting spot and ran away as fast as her legs would take her.

XXX

After a long and very thorough bath in a nearby stream, Alice returned to the campsite. Gronk was back in his loincloth and Waldo had on his robes. Alice got dressed behind some bushes where neither could see, though truthfully she wasn't sure why she even bothered. Through their link, she could tell Waldo was slightly nervous but not at all embarrassed. When she reentered the clearing, Gronk had their packs and all their equipment on his back and was ready to go. Breathing deeply, she rejoined them.

She was calm, completely and totally calm. "All right, I am only going to say this once. Last night and this morning never happened. We will never speak of it again."

"Alice, there is nothing to be embarrassed about, just because you…"

Her left hand grabbed Waldo by the collar and yanked him forward until they were literally nose to nose. Without intending to, the claws of her right hand popped out, so did her tail, which lashed back and forth.

"We NEVER speak of it again. Right?"

Waldo quickly nodded. "Absolutely!"

She let go of her husband. The claws and tail vanished. She took another deep breath, smoothed her blouse and skirt, and gave him a cheerful smile. "Good, now let's get back on the road. I am sure it will be a beautiful day."

XXX

As they walked, Gronk went to Waldo and asked him something in a whisper. "So, Master, what do you do for your birthdays?"

"Well, my family would simply have a small celebration and the giving of gifts. My mother would also offer to grant any single wish within her power."

"Wow. What would you wish for?"

"Cake."

"Nothing else?" the ogre asked in surprise.

Waldo shrugged. "I like cake."

Chapter 9

Blooddrinker

Castle Blooddrinker was unique.

In the city of Alter, here alone plants grew. Within its courtyard existed a small orchard with apple and pear trees, rose bushes, shrubs, ferns, and various other flowers and grasses. These plants could only survive thanks to special magics that provided them light and kept out the black rain.

So much effort merely to keep a fragment of the natural world here, Lilith thought. *Such a waste.*

The Blooddrinkers certainly comprised an unusual lot, even in a place like Alteroth. Their family motto, "From blood, strength" summed up their obsession with breeding and with creating both pure and mixed bloodlines of the different races. There were no pure humans within the clan, branch families included. Every single Blooddrinker had a mixed heritage. Most were partly elven, while some boasted dwarf, goblin, and even werewolf blood. The family kept huge numbers of monster slaves, more than the other six Houses combined. Entire regiments of well-disciplined goblins and orcs served, as well as handfuls of Great Monsters such as ogres, giants, trolls, and medusa. Baldwin's familiar surpassed them all. How the clan acquired Zeruel remained a mystery. A half dragon, the brute proved himself far and away the most dangerous creature in Alteroth. Even Enver would stand no chance against him.

Their obsession extended to their human slaves as well. The clan refused to purchase any but the most attractive and physically gifted. The women were used as breeding stock and given to specifically selected males, not all of whom were human.

The breeding program did not spare the members of the family. Marriages were arranged with an eye to the progeny. Political alliances, money, and love all being of no consequence, what mattered was that the children created from each union be as gifted as possible. Obviously, children with any sort of defect had to be quickly disposed of. Blemishes needed to be cut away to ensure the tree would grow healthy and strong.

Lilith Corpselover was seated with her fellow Council member. Baldwin had extended her an invitation, and she was currently a guest in his home. His troops had escorted her all the way here from her own castle's gate, and when she was done, they would safely return her. Since she had received an open invitation from Baldwin, Lilith knew she was completely safe. If any harm came to her while under his protection, it would be seen as an act of war between their two Houses. She didn't think Baldwin had any ill intentions towards her, but even if he did, he would never act on them while she was his guest. Such a thing would be uncivilized.

The two of them were in a small dining hall enjoying a pleasant meal. Four elven maidens in bright silks of green, blue, red, and gold served them. Such lovely creatures with angelic faces and fluid grace. To the eye, they might appear to be in their early twenties while each could be over a thousand years old. Elves kept their beauty and vitality almost to the end of their lifespans. Only the truly ancient ever showed signs of age. The older Lilith got, the more annoying she found that.

Even more irritating was the way they fawned and smiled at their master. Lilith didn't mind a little obsequiousness from the servants. Propriety demanded it. Their lack of fear was what was so irksome. When they spoke to Baldwin it sounded friendly, like talk between equals. The women had none of the deference you would expect of a servant with her master. And Baldwin actually seemed to encourage it. He smiled at them, called them by name, and even thanked them.

The Blooddrinkers were a strange bunch indeed.

Lilith motioned to the nearest one to fill up her cup. The elf took a pitcher and began to pour. Her hold slipped and a little wine spilled onto Lilith's hand.

Lilith snapped her eyes to the girl and looked at her, simply looked. The servant paled and quickly bowed low, gracefully of course. "I beg your forgiveness, Mistress."

Lilith held out her hand as she turned to Baldwin. The girl took a cloth napkin and dried it as swiftly and gently as she could.

"Your servants don't seem to be very well trained."

"You must forgive, Aelissa," Baldwin said while lowering his face in apology. "You make the girls nervous."

"If they're only nervous, they don't know me very well." She snatched her hand away without bothering to look at the clumsy fool again. "I assume you will punish her."

The girl flinched and backed away, careful to keep her eyes lowered.

"For a little spilled wine? What, would you have me execute her?"

"No, I think a whipping would be sufficient. At least for the first offense."

"Why don't you go, Aelissa? I am sure we'll be able to manage with three attendants."

"Yes, Master Baldwin." She bowed to him and swiftly departed.

"Why do you indulge them so?" Lilith asked. "I have my favorites, too, but I never let them think I will tolerate poor performance."

He smiled at one of the maidens who wore red and had hair the color of polished brass. She smiled back at him. "I love them."

"So? I have fucked plenty of my slaves. It doesn't keep me from punishing them when they deserve it."

"You misunderstand. They are not simply my lovers. I truly care for them and want them to be happy here. They are my sunlight and my night sky. I would never hurt them for something so trivial."

"When you say such things, it makes me think you belong more in Avalon than here."

He gave a soft laugh. "Considering they would view me as an abomination and kill me on sight, I will have to disagree with you."

"Then, maybe you would be happier in Ostagraad, where the monsters reign. You could go to one of the elven kingdoms and frolic in the sunshine. Flowers were never meant to grow here."

"I would be as welcome in the elven lands as I would be in Avalon. They view half elves with disgust and loathing. Elves see humans as being far beneath them, much as you would see a goblin. Like too much of the world, they have no appreciation for what can be achieved by taking the best attributes of different races and melding them together."

"Oh, it must be horribly unfair: humans hate you for being too elven, and the elves hate you for being too human. Life is so very cruel."

Baldwin frowned. "Are you mocking me Lilith?"

"Not at all. My heart is simply filled with sympathy for you."

"How very kind. In any case, this is where I and my family belong. It is the only place where we can be truly accepted. And flowers can grow here; it merely requires some effort."

"Then, I suppose it's really all a question of what you think worth the sacrifice."

Baldwin leaned back into his chair and steepled his fingers. "You asked me for this invitation to my home. What is it you want?"

"Oh, nothing of any great importance. I simply wanted to meet with you as a precaution."

"Precaution for what?"

"In ten days, I will be leaving the city to tour my lands and holdings and visit my relatives."

Baldwin nodded. "Very wise. It is always good policy to introduce the next head of the family to the branch members."

Lilith gave a weary shake of her head. "Hera is not my heir. Part of the reason I am making this trip is to make it clear to everyone. I think they need a reminder of why they fear me. I intend to chop off a few heads and bring the branch families back into line."

"Couldn't you have done something the other day when your relatives were here?"

"What? And ruin the solstice? In any case, it is much better to arrive unannounced. It always unnerves them. You also get to see things with your own eyes. It's dangerous to always rely on reports."

"Is Hera truly not your heir? Why take her as an apprentice, then?"

"My plans for Hera are my own concern. The reason I wanted to meet with you is to give you this warning. I will be absent for about eight weeks. I intend to depart under cover of night and keep my journey as quiet as possible, but it's impossible to be gone for so long and have it not noticed. Darius may see this as an opportunity."

"Even if you are unavailable, he would still need four votes. I doubt he can get them."

"I agree, but the stakes are too high to take unnecessary chances. If Darius does see this as an opening, you are the one most likely to secure Soulbreaker's vote. He would have to try and win over Xilos. He has no hope at all with Gawreth."

"Or with me?"

"You are much too sensible to have any interest in silly adventures."

Baldwin displayed an amused grin. "Why, Lilith. It almost sounds as though we were friends."

"I wouldn't go quite so far. I haven't forgiven you for your part in what happened to my son. But we share a common interest in avoiding a pointless war."

"You can be sure I will be vigilant in your absence and will do all in my power to maintain the peace."

"Good. Your agreement is all I wanted."

XXX

Two days later, a message scrawled on scrap was smuggled out of Castle Blooddrinker. Following secret delivery to a seamstress shop, it was passed onto a servant of one of the Great Houses. The message soon found its way to the hands of Darius Heartless. He read it with a great deal of interest and began making plans.

Chapter 10

Conversations

Alice continually glanced over her shoulder as they traveled the road. Through their connection, Waldo could sense something bothered her.

"What is it?"

"Probably nothing," she said. "But I keep getting this feeling that we're being watched."

"Somebody wants attention," Gronk lisped.

"I am being serious. I keep getting this weird sense we aren't alone."

"Have you actually seen anything?" Waldo asked.

"No, it's probably my imagination."

"Or there could be another possibility." Waldo took out his wand. *"Taranos evel monstri desu noratal est aki est avaratos."*

To Waldo's eyes, a small light came from one of the trees.

XXX

Ikban watched as the magic one used the magic. Ikban did not like the magic or the magic ones. Most of all, Ikban did not like the dead magic one who brought Ikban to this other place. Ikban wanted to go back to where from, to home, but the dead magic one had power over Ikban. Ikban had no choices.

Ikban saw the three go off the road and to trees. Ikban waited then followed, fly Ikban did to other tree. When Ikban get Ikban see only magic one and big green one, no see girl one. Ikban taste air to find. Too late.

XXX

Alice spotted the ugly little thing and leapt out of the bushes. She was in her true form and was able to fly up to the tree branch where the monster was and grab hold of it. "Got you!"

"Skree!" The imp thrashed about and desperately flapped its scaly wings to try and escape. It was only the size of a small dog, though, and Alice had no trouble holding on to him. His body was a greenish brown, with hands and feet both having three clawed digits. When he couldn't get away, he tried to bite her with his fangs.

"Hey! You bite me, and I'll twist your head off!"

The creature didn't pay her warning any mind.

As soon as she caught the little monster, Waldo and Gronk hurried back. Her husband took one look and slowly nodded. "I was afraid of this. It's an imp, a very weak creature but skilled at tracking and remaining hidden. Perfect for pursuing and keeping tabs on people. My grandfather must have summoned him."

"Is that so?" Alice gave the creature a shake. "Did the lich send you?"

"Skree! Skree!"

"Don't bother. Imps can't speak. They're only about as smart as dogs. If you summon one, you can give it commands. Otherwise, they're impossible to communicate with."

"What do we do with it?"

"Kill it. What else? My grandfather will know the moment it dies and send something else to chase us, but we'll have a little leeway at least."

"All right."

Alice casually took hold of the back of the imp's head and twisted his neck until there was a snap, just as she would have done with a squirrel or rabbit. The thing stopped squirming and went limp. Alice tossed it to the ground and wiped her hands.

"Can I eat it?"

"Sure, Gronk."

XXX

"This is a rare sight," Dante Poisondagger said. "Outside of council meetings, it is quite unusual for more than two of us to gather." He, Tiberius Blackwater, and their host Darius Heartless were in a private study within Castle Heartless. He had received an invitation and an urgent request to come here at the second hour past midnight. No reason had been given. Dante was quite suspicious, but he had done good business with Darius in the past and had not wanted to offend. The escort that delivered him here had been quite small in number. No servants to greet him, and he had been led to this place rather than to a dining hall as would be customary. Obviously, Darius was doing his utmost to keep this meeting a secret.

Tiberius smothered a yawn. "I was as surprised as you." He glanced at Darius. "Why are we here?"

"One of my spies learned something very interesting. Lilith Corpselover will be going on an extended tour of her properties. She will be gone from the city for some weeks."

Dante couldn't keep his eyes from widening. "How do you know that? I have multiple spies in the Corpselover household, and they've heard no such thing."

"Apparently she is keeping her plans a secret right up until her departure. My information actually comes from the Blooddrinkers. Lilith had a meeting with Baldwin recently. She is afraid I may try and get a declaration of war again once I know she is gone. Lilith wanted Baldwin to forestall me."

"Will you?" Tiberius asked. "Even if she is gone it still takes four votes. Getting a draw isn't any better than getting voted down."

"The stalemate won't happen again. I'll make sure to secure Xilos's vote prior to the meeting."

"You tried it last time, and he wasn't interested. What makes you think he will listen this time?"

"I can promise him an even greater share of the spoils, as well as a large bribe in gold. Without Lilith here to outbid me, I am sure I can get his support."

"Are you certain Lilith is going on this trip?" Poisondagger asked.

"She told Baldwin directly," Darius replied. "Why would she lie to his face? She would greatly offend him and gain what?"

"I see your point."

"Once she is well and truly gone, I will work quietly on Xilos." He turned to Tiberius. "Would you be willing to offer Soulbreaker a share of the spoils? Gold as well, if you can spare it? Together, we can outbid Baldwin."

"If it helps get us this war, then yes."

"You're going to pay to help Darius get his war?" Dante said in surprise. "What, has he actually won you over with all his insane talk about Avalon and the whites? I didn't realize you were so gullible."

"I don't give a damn about Avalon. I need this war for my own reasons. My position as head of the family is still tenuous. They knelt to me because there was no one else in the main family to offer a challenge. But I am sure some in the branch houses think they can usurp me. I need the glory of a victorious war to firm up support within my House."

"And what happens when the Alliance armies arrive?"

"We crush them!" Darius stated with obvious relish.

Tiberius by comparison did not seem excited by the prospect. "I don't care. I am sure at the very worst we will hold them to a stalemate."

"You've never been to war, Tiberius," Darius said. "If you had ever seen our troops in the field, you would understand. Our forces are massive and battle hardened. The Alliance is nothing but a cloth dragon. They are fearsome to look upon, but they have never had to fight a real war. We will annihilate them!"

Dante was not so sure, but it didn't really matter. Whatever the outcome, he would profit.

"The price is the same as before, one thousand gold skulls. Payable in advance of the vote."

"You should agree to support me without any further payment," Darius said. "I received nothing from you last time."

"I voted to for you, and I argued in your favor at the meeting. You got exactly what was promised. Don't blame me if you couldn't get the last vote you needed."

Darius scowled, but nodded. "You will get your gold."

"Excellent, let's start a war."

XXX

"From now on, I'll cast a detection spell each morning after I renew our wards," Waldo said.

"Is your grandfather really going to keep sending more of those little monsters?" Alice asked.

"He might, or he could use other monsters."

"Like what?"

"Hell hounds, gnolls, snarlaxes, and werewolves. Though werewolves are very hard to summon. He could also use regular animals like hounds or wolves, but if they are bound by a summons, my spell will still detect them."

"And each time we find one we have to kill it?"

"There is no other solution. Once a creature is summoned, it is bound to the will of the summoner. It can only be freed if the master chooses to release control or calls up another creature. The summoner can speak to it magically and can also see through its eyes and know its location."

"So no matter how many of these monsters we kill, more will just keep coming?"

"My grandfather swore to follow me to the ends of the earth. Corpselovers aren't known for giving up easily."

Alice chuckled. "Trust me, darling. I've noticed."

Not long after, Waldo heard a raspy voice whisper.

"Grandson, will you come and talk to me?"

Waldo came to a halt.

"Something wrong, darling?"

"Alice, you and Gronk wait for a bit. I am about to speak with my grandfather."

"He's here?" Her eyes darted about in obvious panic.

"No, no, calm down. I am going to speak to him through a spell."

"I would never tell you your business, Master," Gronk said. "But is gossiping a good idea? Won't it be easier for him to find us now?"

"This spell can't be used for location. In any case, it already has a general idea of where we are."

"Why would you want to talk to that thing anyway?" Alice asked. "It's tried to kill us, and it's still hunting us down."

"True, but we are still family. Not to reply would be impolite. Both of you stay where you are and don't speak."

His familiars nodded, though Alice did not look comfortable. Through the bond, Waldo knew she was much more worried about this than Gronk.

Waldo spoke in the language of magic. *"Yes, I will talk to you."*

Before his face, the image of a hooded skull took shape. Though it was hard to tell, it appeared to be smiling.

"Hello, Grandson."

"Grandfather," Waldo dipped his head slightly.

The skull returned the action. "Still wearing white I see."

"It's necessary."

"It suits you."

"There is no need to be insulting."

The skull chuckled.

"I killed your imp."

"I know, but it took you quite a while. I was able to learn many things in the meantime. I congratulate you on acquiring an ogre. You've taken two Great Monsters on your First Quest. I admit the feat is very impressive."

"Thank you, Grandfather."

"Then, you used your familiars to rescue children and return them to their homes. Truly something a White Mage would do."

Damn it. How embarrassing. "I had my reasons."

"What might they have been? I would have just eaten them. It's not as if children are worth raising as undead. If I were still alive, I would have taken them as slaves. Why did you return them?"

Waldo was not about to admit Alice forced him into it. "I did it to maintain my disguise as a White Mage and spread tales about them. In any case, there are no slave markets in this country. Keeping a herd of unruly children would be inconvenient."

The jaw bone lowered, and there was a hollow laugh. "You are a poor liar, my grandson."

Yes, something I really need to work on. "Maybe I am pretending to be a bad liar in order to misdirect you."

"No, you are truly bad at it. I have much experience with liars. It is well you will never be the head of family. Lying and seeing through the lies of others is an important part of it."

"Was there a specific reason you wanted to speak to me, Grandfather? Or was it only to mock me?"

"Oh, I don't mean to insult you. Truthfully, you have done better than I'd expected. I am beginning to enjoy the hunt. I merely contacted you to ask what you expect to find in Norwich."

"We aren't going to Norwich," Waldo said immediately.

The skull shook from side to side. "Didn't my daughter teach you anything at all about deception? Even if she never thought you would be heir, she should have at least covered the basics."

"We are not going anywhere near Norwich. I knew your imp was there and fed you false information."

"I know where you are going due to your travels the last few days. Your destination is obvious."

Waldo really wished he had a local map so he could name off some other village or town in the area. "Fine, we are going to Norwich, but it's simply to gather supplies. It's not as though anything special is there."

The skull smiled. "One more lie."

"Goodbye, Grandfather. *Nunc.*" He spoke the word of negation, breaking the spell.

As the image faded, the archlich got the last word in. "I look forward to visiting you in Norwich."

Gronk was shaking his head and looking on sympathetically. "The chat didn't go very well, did it, Master?"

"You know, darling, maybe from now on you should avoid talking with anyone or anything that wants to kill you. At the very least, you should let me handle it."

Chapter 11

A Pretty, Pretty Girl

A dozen men on horseback spread out along the road, looking into the woods on either side. Eleven wore chainmail and iron helmets and had either swords or axes. Their leader was in plate armor and carried a lance, as well as a broadsword.

One of the common soldiers nudged his horse and trotted to the knight's side.

"This is a werbil chase if you ask me, Sir Preston. Bunch of stupid villagers making up a crazy story. A White Mage traveling with an ogre and some beautiful woman?" He gave a shake of his head. "If you ask me we might as well go home."

"No one asked you, Sergeant. The duke told us to search and so that is what we'll do."

"Yes, sir, I beg pardon." The sergeant bent his neck and turned his horse around.

After a few more minutes, the knight spurred his mount down the road, and the others followed.

XXX

From their hiding spot in the woods, Waldo, Alice, and Gronk watched them go. He was definitely relieved, fighting twelve well-armed men on horseback would have been much harder than dealing with a pair of goblins. Though potentially, it would have been a chance to fulfill the second part of his quest by defeating a knight.

"It would seem those villagers back in Peabody weren't exaggerating," Waldo said. "The attitude towards monsters seems more severe here than it was in Stratford or Middleton. I suppose you being an ogre might have something to do with it."

"Humans are so petty," Gronk lisped in annoyance. "You eat some of them, and they never get over it."

"You mean as a race, right?" Alice asked. "You haven't eaten any yourself, have you, Gronk?"

The ogre gave a shrug. "Maybe four or five."

Alice stared at him, mouth agape.

"What? They were already dead. Not eating them would have been wasteful. Anyway their skins taste soooooooooo good."

"I really need to learn to stop asking questions."

"Get my backpack, Gronk," Waldo said. "I need to study a spell."

XXX

The three of them remained hidden for the hour or so Waldo spent reading. He was going over some of the spells he had acquired from Roger. As with all the other schools of magic Waldo had studied Illusion back home. Illusionary magic was not viewed as especially valuable. It was actually seen as being less useful than healing. It was a tool for decoration and vanity, of no real importance.

The main problem with illusion was it only had real worth when dealing with mundanes. Mages could sense enchantments, so they were almost never fooled. Waldo was reminded of his own experience with the hedgewizard Roger. Worse, most mages could dispel illusions with ease. *Hopefully we don't run into any.*

When Waldo was satisfied, he shut his spellbook and took out his wand. "Gronk, I'm going to cast an illusion on you so you will appear human."

"You're going to turn me into a cute little human? Really, Master?" Gronk clasped his hands and began twisted from side to side. "Now I can finally talk to the guys and not have them run away."

"I am not changing you into an actual human, Gronk. Doing so would require polymorphication, a deep magic far beyond my means. I will simply cast an illusion on you to make you appear human. Your body will remain exactly the same. Nothing but your image will change."

"So I get to look like a human but still be an ogre? Win!"

"I am glad you are so enthusiastic. Stand still. *"Illusio est imaginem falsam para est illusio."*

The tip of Waldo's wand glowed. So did the outline of Gronk's form. The ogre began to shrink, and his skin color changed. To the naked eye, his entire body warped and twisted. After a short moment, Gronk appeared to be "only" about six and a half feet tall. Rather than pea green, his flesh was dark bronze. He had greasy, uncombed black hair covering the top of his head and a caterpillar-like unibrow above his eyes. There was a wide, bulbous nose and a square jar. Running down the length of the right side of his face was an ugly half-healed scar. More scars and burns splashed his bare chest and thighs. Adorning his shoulders was a lion's pelt which draped over his back, running down to his calves. Mix matched furs wrapped about his hips, draping to the tops of his thighs. Boots made of similar fur adorned his feet and ankles.

Waldo smiled, feeling well satisfied. "Perfect. You look like a barbarian right from the plains of Tarsus or Scythia. Not as intimidating as an ogre, but as much as you could hope for from a human."

Gronk looked over his arms and the rest of his body. "I got little."

"By human standards, you still appear huge. In any case, you remain the same size and weight as before."

"My skin is an ugly color."

"You'll get used to it."

"I want to see what my face looks like."

"Hold on." Alice opened her backpack and dug through it. She pulled out the cook pan. "Here you are."

Gronk took it from her. The bottom was polished well enough to give a clouded reflection. Gronk angled it until he was able to see his new face. He stared into the pan, moving his face from side to side, smiling, frowning, baring teeth, making his eyebrows go up and down, and even playing with his ears and nose. Eventually the ogre tossed the pan aside. "No, it doesn't work for me."

"I know from your perspective it is strange, but you'll get used to looking human."

"Not the problem, Master. I am all right with looking human. I don't want to be a man."

"What?"

Gronk put his hands on his hips and began to swing them around in a circular motion meant, Waldo assumed, to be seductive. It came off as creepy.

"I want to be a girl, a pretty, pretty girl."

Both of Waldo's eyebrows jumped. Of all the things he ever expected to hear come from an ogre's mouth, that was definitely not one of them.

"Why?"

"I just want to know what it feels like to have lots of men want me."

"Trust me, Gronk," Alice said. "It's not so great. They never stop at looking. They always want to touch."

Gronk giggled. "I don't mind."

Waldo shut his eyes and rubbed his temples. *Why do the Dark Powers hate me so?*

"Gronk, you can't be the attractive woman. I already have one of those."

"Thanks, darling. Nice to know I'm appreciated."

"What I mean is I have roles for each of you. Alice is the one who is going to be charming and seductive and win people over. I want you to be intimidating, to make people think twice about causing me any sort of trouble. Looking like a savage from beyond the Inner Sea is perfect for the task."

"Why can't I be the cute one, and she be the scary one? I mean she has the personality for it and all."

Alice immediately punched him in the arm. Hard. "Hey! I am not scary!"

"No, honey, you're a joy." Gronk rubbed his arm. "Let me guess… it's that time of the month isn't it?"

She punched him again, harder.

"See? Scary!"

At this point Waldo thought for the hundredth time his life would be much easier if he had only gotten the contracts right. Familiars were supposed to obey without question. You weren't supposed to have to negotiate with them.

"Gronk," Waldo said, trying to sound patient. "Alice is a succubus. It wouldn't make sense to place an illusion on her to make her appear ugly. It would be a waste of resources. As I keep trying to explain to you, the illusion doesn't affect what you really are. What do you think will happen the first time a man actually tries to grope you?"

"I'll tell him he needs to buy me dinner first, and I like kissing."

The mention of kissing brought back memories. Waldo felt the urge to start spitting as he recalled what an ogre's kiss was actually like. "My point is he will feel the body of an ogre instead of that of a maiden. Which would cause all sorts of problems. Believe me, this is the best solution."

Gronk crossed his arms over his chest and dug in both heels. "I don't care. I want to be a girl."

"Gronk…"

"I said I want to be a girl, girl, girl!" He emphasized the point by slamming a foot down with each "girl."

"Fine," Waldo snapped. "Then I'll make you a girl. *Illusio est imaginem falsam para est illusio.*"

Gronk's apparent height remained exactly the same, as did the skin color. The hair was still greasy, black, and unkempt but was a bit curlier and now went down past the shoulders. The unibrow was kept as was the scar running along the right side of the face. The nose was slightly smaller, while the jaw was rounded. On the chest were two floppy masses about the size of cantaloupes. They and most of the chest were bound up in a black leather girdle with brass studs. There was a short skirt also made of black leather, bronze greaves on the ankles, and sandals. Scars crisscrossed both the thighs and arms, and the body itself remained very muscular. The result was about as unfeminine and unattractive as a healthy woman's body could be.

"There, is this better?" Waldo demanded.

Gronk held out his arms and then stared down at his new body. He picked up the pan to get a look at his new face. He stared at it for a long while. Eventually he turned to Waldo. "Thank you, Master!"

"Huh?"

"I am sooooooooo beautiful! I mean look at these breasts… and this ass and all these cute scars! They aren't going to be able to look away from me." He smirked at Alice. "Don't be mad when all the men stop paying attention to you."

"I don't think it will be a problem."

I guess being an ogre he doesn't truly understand human standards in beauty. "Well, I am glad everything is resolved."

"Oh, there's just one more thing. I need a girly name now. You know, for when we are in public."

"Did you have something in mind?"

"Belle," Gronk said immediately. "It was the name of this sweet little shepherd girl I ate once."

"Fine, it's a perfect name for a five-hundred-pound ogre. All right, in public your name will be Belle."

Chapter 12

Worth A Chance

Celton Poisondagger sat forty-fifth on the left side of the table, literally as far from his father as it was possible to be and still be seated. Celton was with the children who were too young to be apprenticed. When the adults further up the table turned in his direction, there were mocking smiles and shakes of heads. He had fallen so completely out of his father's favor no one felt the need to even pretend to respect him. Pyrus, Fenwyk, and Murat were openly pleased. So far as they were concerned, he was no longer a rival for the succession.

When the servants led him to this chair, Celton had been sure it was some sort of mistake. He had done all of his father's dirty work for years and nothing to deserve this sort of humiliation. Places at the table changed all the time but not like this. Celton went directly to the head of the House and demanded to know the reason for his drastic demotion.

Dante was all too happy to tell him. "You're a fool. The family incomes have been shrinking for years, our treasury in near empty, and everywhere you look there is corruption. I trusted you to handle the family business, and this is the result. Obviously you're not fit for important matters. Go and sit with the grandchildren. It's where you belong."

The absolute injustice of the words made him want to choke!

Corruption everywhere you looked? Well of course! Every branch family put its own financial interests ahead of those of the main family. They no longer feared Father. They understood he had no interest in keeping a tight rein any more. His only preoccupation was with his own selfish pleasures. If the system still worked at all was due to Celton's own efforts. Sudden inspections, and the occasional execution, were the only things keeping any revenue coming in. It was not enough. He could not check every account and transaction, and most of the branch families had the sense not to be too blatant. That House Poisondagger was not already bankrupt was due to him.

The family faced financial ruin because of his father. Yet knowing there was a shortage of funds, Dante continued to spend as lavishly as ever. Father acted in the manner of a spoiled child who demanded every whim be fulfilled and never cared about what it cost. At this rate in just one or two more years, the family coffers would be empty.

What then when they could no longer afford to equip and feed their soldiers? When they could not afford to buy slaves or raw materials in other lands? When they could no longer purchase goods from the other Houses? Among the Seven Great Families, it was vital to never show weakness, not only to the outside world but to one another. What greater weakness could there be than to have to admit you were coinless?

When the time came, they would have to find a new source of money merely to maintain themselves. Some wealthy nations that loans to kings and other important men. Venezia and

Trezibon came immediately to mind. But going to foreigners to beg for help was unthinkable! Within Alteroth there were no banks or merchant houses to offer loans. Each Great House handled those functions themselves. The family would have no choice but to turn to one of the other Houses. At which point, House Poisondagger would become nothing more than a puppet. They would belong to one of the other families and be used the way a man used a pretty slave girl.

If things did not change a terrible reckoning was coming. Celton had been working tirelessly to stave it off. But it felt hopeless, because this bleak future was brought on by the one man who controlled Poisondagger's fate. So long as his father lived, all his efforts were in vain. Now, as the final insult, his father made him the scapegoat for all of it. Dante washed his hands of the mess he created and laid all the blame at Celton's feet.

Celton could do nothing about it.

He wanted to curse and scream at the disgusting old man, to defend himself and call his father out on all the stupidity and greed about to bring them to ruin. But he knew it was pointless. No one cared if he was innocent. All that mattered to anyone was he had fallen. To the rest of the family, it was good news.

So he did the only thing he could. He clamped his mouth shut and ate his dinner.

XXX

A couple hours after the meal, a servant came to his quarters and informed he was summoned to his father's study.

Celton wondered if the order called him to his own execution. It would not be the first time Father decided to humiliate one of his children before putting that person to death. If it was the case, most of the family would be gathered to bear witness. The thought of escape briefly flickered through his mind. If the guards knew, Celton had little chance to get out of the castle alive. I he tried, all his children would be executed. There was nothing to do but go and meet his fate.

When he arrived, no one from the family greeted him. Two guards waited outside his father's door. Celton was actually surprised. He entered. Father sat behind his desk, a goblet of wine in one hand. Dante waited until the guard shut the door to speak. "You look upset my son. Something at dinner not agree with you?"

Celton deliberately clamped his jaw shut to avoid yelling and cursing. His father had the power of life and death and not one to be very tolerant. "Why?" he finally spat.

His father smiled with those rotten teeth. "Did it hurt your pride? It must have. To go from my most trusted helper to the family fool. I could see the fury on your face. If you had pulled out a wand, it wouldn't have surprised me."

Beware the vengeance of a patient man, was one of the many sayings Celton had been taught growing up. "How many of the others have already come to you about taking my place?"

His words brought a snort of laughter. "All of them, of course. I know you were too far away to hear, but the food was barely on the table before some of them were promising to do a much better job of running things."

"I noticed Pyrus was waving his hands about even more than usual."

"He was the most aggressive and loudest. The others were slightly more subtle. But all of them were desperate to win me over."

Both Celton's hands were balled into fists, and he could not keep a slight tremor from his voice. "I know you don't like many of the things I said and did, but I am not incompetent. You don't hear the truth very often. It's only natural you wouldn't care for it. Whoever you choose to take my place will surely tell you what you want to hear and rob the House blind."

"I'm sure you never stole a single copper knuckle."

"I took a little gold here and there." It was true, and Father would never believe it if he pretended otherwise. Celton was loyal to the family and hard working. He was not a saint or an idiot. "But much less than I could have and much less than anyone else would have. It was nothing compared to how much I saved you."

"If you did such a wonderful job, why is my vault near empty?"

"How much did you spend for all the silk from Trezibon?" They both knew the answer: three hundred gold skulls.

His father's smile vanished. Dante really was not used to being on the receiving end of any sort of criticism, even when it was veiled. "It doesn't matter. I am the head of a Great House. I can have whatever I want."

As if your outrageous spending had nothing to do with the fact your vault is empty.

"All you ever bring me are complaints and problems. Every time you want to talk, it's to deliver more trouble."

"Only because our House is consumed with rot!"

"Then you should have fixed things yourself. It's what I expected."

"I did! But you only gave me enough authority to fix the small problems. When I came to you about the big ones, you always ignored me."

Dante narrowed his eyes. "So you do think this is my fault."

Celton knew better than to answer the challenge directly. "I took care of what I could and told you about the things I couldn't. Whoever it is you pick to replace me will simply tell you everything is wonderful while our House falls to ruin."

"Well, for now, no one will replace you."

"Want to see who begs the most?"

Celton's question earned another chuckle. "I see enough begging every day. Besides, if things go well, I may not replace you at all. Try and smile a bit, my son. Your exile to the far end of the table may be short."

"What do you mean?" Celton asked warily.

"I am going to share a secret with you."

"You're going to trust me?" *Trust is a dagger pointed at your own heart*, was another of the sayings he learned as a boy.

"Only a little. It's a very important secret, but not one that can be kept for long. You will not share it."

"Of course."

"Through sources I have confidence in, I have learned Lilith Corpselover had a meeting with Baldwin Blooddrinker. She informed him she would be leaving the city to tour her lands."

Celton saw the significance immediately. "The same news Enver delivered. You didn't believe the vampire."

"Why would I? He could have easily been acting under Lilith's orders. Hearing the same from a different source makes it much more credible. Still not certain but worth a chance at least."

"You wish me to meet with him?"

His father nodded. "Before I will agree to anything, I will interrogate the vampire myself and know whether or not he is lying."

"He warned we have many Corpselover spies in our household," Celton said quickly. "Enver specifically advised only you and I should know about this. If it goes beyond the two of us, Lilith will certainly find out."

"I don't need you to tell me we have spies. You can inform Enver we will meet in secret, only the three of us. *If* it turns out he is speaking the truth, we will make the attempt on Lilith's life. Make sure the vampire understands that I will be using a Circle of Truth on him. Be certain to explain if he is lying, he will not leave this castle alive. Destroying her familiar would be no small achievement."

"I will make it most clear to him, Father."

"You may need to contact him more than once to arrange the meeting. Even if it is in the early hours, someone might notice your comings and goings. Fortunately, no one will care about it now."

Celton's eyes suddenly opened wide. "Is that why you humiliated me? To make it easier to make arrangements unnoticed?"

His fury only made his father smile again. "What? Do you think your fragile pride is more important to me than the chance to kill Lilith?"

"You didn't have to go so far!"

"I'll decide how far to go with things. Now leave me. As things stand, we may only have a week or so before she departs. There is no time to waste."

Celton wanted to storm out and get as far away from his cursed forebearer as possible. But as had happened so often before, his sense of duty to the family made him stay. He already knew his effort would not be appreciated.

"There was an important matter I was going to bring up with you. If I am still the family overseer, then I need to discuss it."

His father took a quick gulp of wine and set the goblet down. His lips became a short thin line, and his face went rigid. The way Dante's eyes squeezed nearly shut spoke only of annoyance. Celton was familiar with this pose. He saw it whenever he brought Father news he did not want to hear. "What is it?"

"Two more city guards have been murdered in Pontian. They make nine in the last two months. From the report, these were particularly gruesome. The bodies were sliced open from shoulder to crotch, and the organs were pulled out for display."

"What do I care? That damn city is nothing but a sinkhole. It costs me more to run than it brings in. I am sick of hearing about it."

Of course you are. It's a problem and a very bad one. "Crime there is getting completely out of hand. The local police force isn't even pretending to deal with it anymore. The Children of Liberty are growing more brazen by the day."

Dante gave a snort. "Children of Liberty, fancy name for a bunch of thieves and killers."

"These criminals are getting dangerously popular. The locals love them, far more than they do us."

"As if I would ever want to be loved by my slaves. Let them hate, so long as they fear."

"The problem, Father, is they are starting not to. From sunset to sunrise, the city belongs to the criminals. Our guards lock themselves in their stations. They won't patrol at night any more. Our own men are beginning to fear the Children more than us."

"Then kill them and get new men."

"We don't have enough guards in our other holdings to replace them. Are you willing to pay for raising and training a brand new garrison?"

The hard look his father sent him was all the answer he needed. "Schlek needs to be removed as governor. He's incompetent and has no idea what to do."

"No, I've told you before, he is married to Appalla, the oldest from Anora, my third wife. She is a sweet girl, and I'm fonder of her than I am of you. I'm not forcing her from the governor's palace because some thieves killed a few guards."

That "sweet girl" was forty-seven, the mother of six, and had a fondness for beatings.

"If you won't remove Schlek, then let me assign him a special overseer. We can raise five hundred soldiers and give them to someone ruthless who knows what he is doing. Send Murat to clean the city. I'm sure he'd have plenty of enthusiasm for the task. Let the streets run with blood for a few weeks, and everything will be better."

Dante lifted an eyebrow. "You'd actually give your younger brother a chance to impress me?"

"The situation is serious and needs a hard hand. My brother is very competent and thorough. Give him the manpower he needs, and he will clear this mess up."

"Do you have any idea how expensive it is to call out five hundred soldiers?"

"It's still cheaper than having to put down another revolt."

"They wouldn't dare!" Dante snapped. "They know what we do to rebels… we would massacre the whole lot and burn the place to the ground. These sort are always cowards. Brave enough to steal and murder when they know they can get away with it, they wouldn't be stupid enough to actually rebel."

"It wouldn't be the first time. We've had riots and rebellions before."

"And we've put every one of them down. We emptied out the towns and villages where they took place. We've made examples."

"Yes," Celton said patiently. "And all those places are still empty. They raise no crops and produce no revenues. Plus, it's always expensive to send in soldiers and mages to slaughter our own people. We gain nothing from it."

"What we gain is a reputation for not tolerating rebellion."

"The people don't seem to have learned the lesson."

"Then, we'll teach it as many times as we have to."

"Pontian is a large city. Putting down a full revolt there would be very costly, and we would lose a lot of assets. Actually destroying the city would be a disaster for us."

"Still better than looking weak."

"Please don't forget Pontian is right on the border with Dregal. I am certain they are encouraging events. The situation has the potential to be a disaster. Let me send Murat with five hundred men and cure the sickness before it becomes any worse."

"Don't worry about Dregal. Their time is coming. Stop bringing Pontian up to me. I don't want to hear any more about it. The place is a pit, and I am not going to throw away my gold trying to fix it. Tell Schlek he can raise twenty more guards. They should be enough to hold the line."

"It won't be."

"Enough. Too much in fact. I have had my fill of complaints from you. Your only worry is the vampire. Now, leave me."

"Yes, Father." Celton bowed and departed.

As hard as it was to imagine, Celton thought he might be even unhappier returning to his quarters than he had been leaving them.

Chapter 13

Norwich At Last

"I would say I made the right choice," Waldo said.

"Sure seems like it, Master."

After all of their diversions, they finally arrived at the city of Norwich. It was encased by a twenty-foot-high stone wall without any towers. Along the wall, about twenty feet apart, were wooden pikes. On top of each was a turnip shaped skull. Most were nothing but bleached bone. The ones directly above the gate still had some meat on them. From their condition, they looked to have been rotting for weeks.

"They really don't like goblins, do they?" Alice asked.

"I'm thinking they don't much like any of us monsters," Belle said.

"It is terrible." Waldo nodded. "They could have been made into slaves. So much good labor wasted."

"They were probably all killed in fighting," Alice said. "The ones they capture get sold. This is where most of the goblins in Middleton come from."

"You really think you're going to find another monster here, Master? Don't seem too likely."

"Whatever the attitude of the locals, I believe I will. The map I was given told me where to find you and Alice. No reason to think it won't be right a third time."

A few miles beyond the city, the marshlands began. Those territories belonged to the goblins. You would find no farms or human settlements within them. Norwich effectively marked the frontier in Lothas. As such, there was only one road into the city and a single gate. A pair of fifteen-foot tall iron doors stood open with about a dozen well-armed soldiers standing watch. No moat or abatis surrounded the city, though soldiers patrolled the top of the wall and kept an eye out. Waldo didn't find the defenses particularly impressive, but he supposed they didn't need to be to hold off goblins. The creatures were strong and savage but not very intelligent. They were incapable of siege tactics or of building catapults or other such weapons.

Inside the gate stood a pole with a banner fluttering about in a light breeze. It depicted some sort of winged creature with a bird's head and lion's legs all in gold on a field of crimson. In the middle of the creature's body was a red heart.

The instant Alice got a clear look at it her eyes widened. "Oh, damn it," she whispered.

Belle glanced in her direction, but Waldo missed it completely as the sergeant in charge of the gate approached. He and the other soldiers gawked at them. The one in charge at least remembered his manners and bowed. "Welcome to Norwich, Master."

Waldo gave a slight nod in return. "I am the great Waldo Rabbit. This is my wife Alice Rabbit and my bodyguard Belle of Tarsus."

The sergeant offered bows to both. Alice didn't appear to notice, while Belle giggled and gave a wave with one hand.

"Duke Theos Griffinheart offers you his hospitality. If you like, I can have one of my men take you to his keep."

"No need," Waldo said. "I prefer to stay at an Inn."

The man's features went slack, obviously surprised by the answer. "Are you certain, Master Rabbit? It is custom for visiting White Mages to stay at the Duke's residence."

"I have my reasons. We White Mages are a mysterious bunch. It's because we are plotting to take over the world."

Both the sergeant's eyebrows rose.

"My husband and I definitely prefer to stay at an Inn," Alice added while looking intently into the man's eyes. "I hope that is not a problem?"

He swayed slightly on his feet. "No, no problem at all. I hope you enjoy your stay."

Waldo sent Alice a momentary glance. "Tell me, are there any monsters in this city?"

"Monsters? No, they are forbidden. The ones our patrols catch get put in stock pens until they can be sold. The only monsters you'll find inside the walls are at the end of pikes."

"I see."

"You heard him, darling." Alice grabbed his arm and began dragging him away. "No monsters here. I guess we should leave."

"What? Alice, we're not going yet! We just arrived, and we are going to investigate this place." He tried digging in his heels but she kept pulling him along.

Belle took Alice by the scruff of her neck, lifting her off the ground with one hand.

"Hey!" Alice glared furiously at Belle and tried to kick "her." Alice's feet flailed in the air.

"Now, come on, sweetie. Don't pout. If master says we're staying, we're staying. Anyway, I want to see if there are any cute guys in this place."

XXX

As the strangers entered the city, the sergeant couldn't take his eyes from the beautiful red haired woman. Despite his sudden infatuation, he did send one of his men to inform the duke of their new arrivals. One to keep track of them, as well.

XXX

Waldo decided the best place to begin the search would be in the middle of Norwich. As they walked along the streets, people stared wide-eyed and made sure to keep a safe distance. A few made sketchy bows towards him, most simply gawked and quickly got out of the way. It was about how the mundanes had treated him in Middleton. They still weren't looking at him with the proper amount of fear, but it was close enough.

As they went, Belle waved at nearly every man they passed. The reactions tended to range from confusion to glassy-eyed disbelief to putting heads down and swiftly walking away. Belle gave Alice a nudge with his elbow. "Try not to hate me."

"What?" Her eyes had been darting about nervously.

Belle put both hands behind his back and skipped, making the ground shake. "I'm the one all the men will look at."

"Somehow I doubt it, but believe me, you're welcome to the attention. The last thing I want is to be noticed."

"Is that so?" Waldo glanced at her over his shoulder. "Why did you use your Charm then?"

Alice put her hands together and slowly wrung them. "I didn't want him to press us on staying with the duke. I really want to get out of this city."

"I see."

"I am sorry for using my Charm without telling you."

"I don't mind, Alice. In fact I would prefer you to use it more often."

"You know I won't."

"Except for today?"

Her hands moved more intensely. "I don't want to draw extra attention."

Belle snorted. "Right, who would notice a White Mage and a couple beauties like us?"

Alice's eyes darted about once more. "So long as it's not the wrong person who sees."

XXX

The middle of the city turned out to be the market district. An empty field contained tents and stalls crowded together. There were local farmers shouting from the backs of wagons about eggs or vegetables or about freshly slaughtered chickens or pigs. Women sold pies and bread. There was ale, tobacco, cheese, cloth, tools, and all other sorts of goods, all hawked by people exhorting their grand quality and value. A crowd steadily meandered through, filling the empty spaces between the stalls and tents.

Wherever Waldo went the crowds parted, and an empty area appered. People stopped to stare and make sure to keep a safe distance. Waldo tried his best to ignore them. Belle reveled in the attention and was nothing but smiles. Alice seemed distinctly uncomfortable.

"This should do." Waldo took out his wand and intoned the words to a spell. As he did so people gasped and pushed further away. "*Taranos evel monstri desu noratal est aki est avaratos.*"

The detection spell was completed Waldo was rewarded with... nothing. Not so much as a glimmer of magical light came from anywhere. Not even from Alice and Belle due to the protective wards he'd placed on them. He did not lose all hope, as Norwich was a very flat location, and he could not get a clear view of all of it at once.

But Great Monsters gave off a tremendous glow. In Stratford he'd had no trouble at all finding Alice. She was over a mile away and inside a building, but the light coming off of her had been so powerful it had been impossible to miss. The only reason he'd so much trouble finding Gronk was due to the light from a horde of goblins masking that of a single ogre. In a city empty of other monsters Waldo would have expected a clear sign if there really were a Great Monster here.

He was not about to give up, but it was a discouraging start.

"Well?" Alice asked. "Please tell me you've found what we came here for."

"No, I'm afraid not. There's no sign of it."

"A shame, darling." She patted his shoulder. "Still, you did your best, so I guess we can leave now?"

"Don't be ridiculous. You know how much time and effort I put into finding Gro... Belle. I won't do any less now."

"Wonderful," she sighed.

"Why are you so fearful?"

"What do you mean?"

"I've been sensing it through our bond ever since we arrived. I know being in a strange city can be a bit unnerving, but I've never felt this much anxiety from you before."

"I don't know what you mean, darling. I'm not nervous at all. I am completely fine, as relaxed as can be."

"Alice…"

"I said I'm fine!"

Waldo possessed no extraordinary skills at reading people, but even to him the lie was obvious. Under a normal contract a familiar wouldn't be able to lie to her master. Having somehow botched the contract though Waldo was stuck trying to deal with her more or less as an ordinary husband might.

Dark Powers help him.

"I know what the problem is," Belle announced. "It's obvious."

Alice turned to him apprehensively. "You do?"

Belle nodded. "You're upset because you're the ugly one now."

"Yes," Alice said in a flat voice. "You got me."

"Come on," Waldo said. "Let's search and see if we can find anything."

XXX

As they went through the marketplace, people kept moving out of the way. At least most did. A man was hurrying in the other direction and ran straight on into Alice.

"Eek!" Without thinking she instinctively punched him in the chest, knocking him down.

"Ow!" he was sprawled out in front of her, rubbing where she had hit him. She immediately regretted it. He obviously hadn't done it on purpose. "I'm sorry I'm sorry. I didn't mean to hit you so hard." Alice held a hand out.

He took it, spryly getting back to his feet. He looked like a farmer, with a ratty old cloak, brown tunic, and weather beaten breeches. The man had curly auburn locks, mysterious gray eyes, and an attractive face. She noticed his hand was quite soft.

As quick as he was up he managed to press his lips to her hand. "Quite all right, my dear lady. Small price to pay for meeting such a beauty."

Alice yanked it back. "I'm glad you're not hurt."

"So am I." He gave her a mischievous grin. "If you will excuse me, I must go. I hope to see you again." He then hurried past and was swallowed up by the crowd.

"Do you normally throw men down on the ground when you meet them, sweetie?" Belle asked.

"Oh, be quiet. I don't like being touched by a man."

"Could have fooled me. I've heard you moaning."

Alice could feel her face get hot. Didn't Gronk have any shame at all? "Waldo is the only exception. I don't mind when he touches me."

"I sort of got the idea from the moaning."

"We're wasting time," Waldo said in annoyance.

It only took four or five steps for Alice to notice a weight at her hip was missing. She looked at her waist. The drawstring tying her purse to her had been neatly cut. "We've been robbed!" She understood immediately what must have happened. "That man who bumped into me! Thief!" Alice turned and ran back in the other direction. "Out of the way! Thief! Stop thief!"

Folks stepped aside to clear a path but not quickly enough. Alice pushed them out of her way. Belle was at her side doing the same. Waldo was followed in their wake. There were shouts and confusion as she pushed and manhandled her way through until they were clear of the market. They found themselves in an empty street. Alice looked around desperately but could not spot any sign of the man.

"I don't see him anywhere."

"Me neither," Belle said.

She turned desperately to Waldo. "Darling, isn't there something you can do with your magic?"

"There is no such thing as a detect thief spell, and I have no connection to him. So scrying magic won't work, even if I had any of those spells memorized to begin with."

"So he's gone?" she cried in despair. "He took all our money! We don't have a single coin now, nothing!"

"I see. Then, I don't suppose we can afford an Inn. It looks like we'll have to accept the duke's hospitality after all."

The thought of meeting Theos Griffinheart made her stomach turn to lead. "Uh, we still have our tents and blankets. Why don't we stay in a nice quiet alley?"

Chapter 14

Duke Theos Griffinheart

It was surprisingly easy to gain access to the duke's keep. A few questions to the locals had given them the general directions. When they arrived they were ushered into the reception hall and told the duke would be with them soon. Hanging down from the far wall were three banners like the one that had been at the gate.

Alice stared up at them.

She had done everything she could think of to talk Waldo out of coming here. He was adamant about remaining in Norwich until he either found his third monster or was absolutely convinced there wasn't one. Since they were now coinless, they would have to accept the local ruler's hospitality. Alice had offered to work to pay for their room and board, as she had back in Middleton. Waldo though wanted to find his monster as quickly as possible, and thought the duke might be of help.

In the end she hadn't been able to convince him. As a last resort she'd considered telling him why she wanted nothing to do with this lord. She was ashamed of her past and didn't want to bring it up. It was bad enough she was not human, she didn't want to remind him that she'd almost been another's property. Alice would hope and pray that she would go unnoticed.

Alice noted that Waldo had wandered over to some of the furnishings and decorations. He was giving special attention to an engraved chest with silver metalwork. She went over to keep a closer eye on him.

"What are you doing?"

"The quality isn't too bad," Waldo said looking closely at the chest. "Not as good as what my family has, but not bad, all things considered."

"Please, please tell me you're not thinking about doing something stupid."

"Don't be insulting Alice, when have I ever done anything stupid?"

"Do you actually want a list?"

He frowned at her and she could sense annoyance through their bond. "I am not going to do anything right this moment. That doesn't mean I am not going to take inventory for later."

"We are guests here," Alice looked about. There were only two guards at the other end of the hall and well out of earshot. Even so she lowered her voice. "Don't they have guest rights and laws of hospitality where you come from?"

"Certainly, very strict ones. If a House sends you an open invitation, and you accept, you are under their protection. If any harm comes to you it is considered a huge insult to the other House and an act of war. No Great House would ever harm a guest who had accepted an open invitation, they would be seen as outcasts by the other Houses. The guest is forbidden to inflict any harm on their host or their host's family or household. Violating that law isn't quite as heinous as the other, and is not an act of war, but it would still be seen as a very great disgrace."

"That… that actually sounds enlightened."

"You seem surprised."

"Well, and please don't take this the wrong way, but your people have a reputation for being immoral."

"Oh we are, completely and utterly, that doesn't mean we're not civilized. In fact we consider ourselves to be the *only* civilized nation."

"That's very arrogant darling."

He shrugged. "We can't help it if we're superior to everyone else."

She shut her eyes and shook her head slightly. *Why do I even try?* She loved him and had no doubts that he was a good person, in his own way. But some of his ideas were very hard to deal with. "Well since we are guests here I take it that means you aren't going to try to steal anything. Right?"

"Well not unless I am sure I can get away with it."

"What happened to not doing any harm to your host? Or does robbing him not count?"

"The laws of hospitality and guest rights only apply if the head of one of the Seven Great Houses extends an open invitation to a member of one of the other Houses. If the invitation is secret, extended by anyone other than the head of the family, or is sent to anyone who is not a member of one of the Houses those rules do not apply. Since I am in a foreigner's home I am under no obligation to him."

"So you only play nice with the people you know?"

"I would never describe it as, 'nice' but, essentially, yes."

"You know I would have thought that what happened to us would have at least shown you why it's wrong to steal. We lost all our money because of some damn thief. Can you see the lesson in that?"

"Certainly, from now on I should hold our coins, or maybe Gronk should."

"Belle," the disguised ogre said.

"Only when other people can hear us."

"That's the wrong lesson darling," Alice tried to sound patient. "Stealing is wrong. You shouldn't take what isn't yours. Being the victim now can't you see that?"

"It's only wrong when you are the victim. It's just fine so long as you are the one doing the robbing."

Belle nodded. "I like the way Master thinks."

"You be quiet," she stabbed a finger at Belle and then at Waldo. "And you, forget about stealing anything. You don't want to do that. Griffinhearts are bad people. They're arrogant and vindictive and think they can have anything they want. Even if you think we can get away with it, just don't. Trust me, we don't want to make an enemy out of this family."

"Really? How do you know so much about them?"

"Ah, well they're very famous. They're rich and they're related to the ruling house." She began wringing her hands again.

"How rich?"

"Don't, we have enough problems as it is."

XXX

The Duke at last arrived to formally welcome his guests.

He was dressed in shining plate mail, though the chest piece looked to be in danger of snapping off. The Duke was a big, broad shouldered man with thick arms and legs. Undoubtedly in his younger days he had been an impressive figure. He still was, but had a large belly and double chin. Behind him trailed several servants and two more guards.

Waldo saw his eyes flash first to him and then Belle. It was Alice that held his gaze.

The duke came over to him and gave a slight nod of his head. Waldo returned the gesture.

"Welcome to Norwich Master Rabbit. I, Duke Theos Griffinheart, offer you the comfort and security of my home for the length of your stay."

Though the man was addressing him his eyes kept wandering over to Alice.

"I thank you for your kind invitation and wish you Unity, Justice, and Peace and all that."

"I've had a few White Mages visit over the years, but they always travelled alone. Won't you introduce me to your companions?"

Before Waldo could reply Belle leaned forward with a huge smile. "I am Belle of Tarsus, you cute pudgy man you."

"Er, yes, a pleasure I am sure." Griffinheart turned and stepped in front of Alice. His eyes were sliding up and down her body as his fingers impatiently danced.

She gave a smooth curtsy, then spoke, almost sang. "My Lord, I am Mrs. Alice Rabbit."

"You're his wife? Truly?" There as a regretful sigh. "Ah, what a terrible shame, I suppose Lancel wasn't quick enough."

"What?! I mean... I don't know what you are referring to my Lord."

"You are Alice, the barmaid from that whorehouse in Stratford aren't you?"

Her eyes bulged out and her mouth opened and closed soundlessly.

"How do you know about that?" Waldo asked.

"My son was smitten by her. He described her to me in great detail. Her fire colored hair, the eyes of amethyst, her huge... heart."

Alice crossed her arms over her bosom. "Yes, men are always noticing my heart."

"Ah, that's right, Elsa mentioned to me there was someone else who wanted to buy you." Waldo said.

"Luckily Elsa was always greedy, otherwise I would have been sold off before we ever met."

"I am sure you would have been happy to have belonged to my son."

Alice took a hold of Waldo's arm. "I am happier being married to my husband."

"No doubt, no doubt," he looked at Waldo. "You truly are a lucky man."

"I know."

"If you are still here when my son returns I am sure he will tell you the same."

Waldo felt her grip tighten and a surge of fear through their bond.

"La... Lancel is coming here?"

Duke Griffinheart grinned. "No need to look so frightened. I am sure my son will be disappointed, but he is not going to try and steal you away."

"No, of course he wouldn't."

Waldo could tell her fear was growing. He wasn't sure why. He had bought her after all, and the people of this land seemed to respect private property.

"Duke Griffinheart," Waldo said. "The reason I've come here is that I am looking for a monster."

"You've come to the right place then. Go into the marshes and you'll find thousands of them, like rats in a sewer. No matter how many we catch or kill the damn things just keep breeding."

Waldo felt anger flare in both of his familiars.

"I am not interested in common goblins. I've heard there was a Great Monster here in Norwich."

"Inside my city?" The duke shook his head, making his chins wobble. "Whoever told you that was a damn liar. I don't tolerate such disgusting things here. The people in Middleton and other places may put up with such repulsive filth, but I assure you that I don't."

"Not all monsters are disgusting," Alice snapped. "They don't all deserved to be killed either, not just for being what they are."

Griffinheart gave her the sort of smile you might offer to a small child babbling nonsense. "Dear girl, I am sure the goblins in Stratford are very tame. Perhaps some of them do tricks. Here, we understand what they truly are. They aren't pets or oxen, they are monsters in every sense of the word. If it weren't for the money from the traders we would kill every last one we could. Believe me, they don't deserve any sort of pity. I am sure your husband feels exactly the same way."

"Being a White Mage that goes without saying. So there are really no monsters anywhere in Norwich?"

"None."

"What about in the area?"

"As I said, thousands."

"I mean Great Monsters; vampires, giants, dragons. Are there any creatures like that close by?"

The duke hesitated for just a moment. "No, there are only goblins."

"You're sure?"

"Quite sure, Master Rabbit. Now I am certain you are weary from your travels. Let us have a meal together. Please enjoy my hospitality for as long as you care to."

Chapter 15

A Dagger Pointed At Your Own Heart

They shared a very pleasant meal with their host.

Belle ate enough for five. Waldo asked questions about local geography and recent monster activity. Alice tried to remain quiet. She was forced to answer a number of questions from the duke, who paid her far more attention than he did to Waldo. Following this, some servants brought them to the quarters they would be staying at. The duke was generous enough to give Belle separate accommodations, so that Waldo and his wife could enjoy some privacy.

Almost as soon as they were alone, Alice began to pace. Short, quick strides took her from one end of the room to the other.

"We should leave here as soon as we can," Alice said, never slowing her gait. "Tonight, or in the morning at the very latest. Lord Griffinheart doesn't know when his son will be back, so we should get as far away from here as we can."

"We can't leave until we find my third familiar," Waldo said. "Why are you so afraid?"

"Because Lancel will kill me."

"Because you are mine now? Seems rather petty."

"You don't understand. He's not the sort of man who takes no for an answer. Every time he came to the inn, he got a little more forceful, a little more impatient. He doesn't like to lose. I think he would rather have me killed than see me with another man. I'm assuming he hasn't found out the truth. Lancel would definitely kill me, then. He likes monsters about as much as his father does."

"I still don't see why you're so worried. He's only human."

His words brought her to a sudden halt to gawk at him. "So was the crowd that threw you in the river."

"Hmmm," Waldo replied. "Good point."

"Then, we can go?"

"No, we can't leave until I'm sure there's no Great Monster here."

"So you'd rather put my life in danger?" Her hands waved about. "Darling, Lancel might decide to kill you, too, out of jealousy or because he suspects the truth."

"It doesn't make a difference, Alice. We are already in danger. My grandfather knows we're in Norwich. I am sure Melissa is searching for us, as well."

"Then why don't we just go?"

"Getting a third Great Monster is worth the risk. They are very hard to acquire. Once we leave there is no guarantee I will ever be able to get another. The conditions of my quest are close to impossible. I need every conceivable advantage."

"What happens if Lancel shows up here tomorrow?"

"His father has no idea when he'll return. The odds of it being tomorrow seem slim."

"What if he appears anyway?"

"Then I'd say our best chance for survival is for you to Charm him the moment you see him."

She planted her hands on her hips. "And if that doesn't work?"

"Then we'll have to fight our way out of the city."

"If it comes to that we'll be slaughtered!"

"Then let's hope it doesn't prove necessary."

Alice shut her eyes and took a couple deep breaths. Through the bond, Waldo could feel her fear diminishing somewhat, while her frustration mounted.

"How can you be so calm about this?"

"Because it doesn't really change our situation. I understand we are in danger, but we would be regardless. What do you suppose will happen if my grandfather arrives at the gate? Or Melissa? Things would be as bad or worse."

"Fine. If we're staying no matter what, then I think you should know the duke was lying when you asked him about monsters in the area."

"Are you certain?"

"Pretty much. I have a lot of experience with men telling lies. One of the benefits of being a barmaid."

"Interesting." Waldo gave her his full attention and narrowed his eyes.

"What?"

"You were holding this back until I made it clear we weren't leaving. If I had decided to go, you wouldn't have told me at all, would you?"

Her eyes darted towards the floor, and she tugged at her hair.

"I was going to tell you," she mumbled.

"You also didn't mention Lancel until the duke brought him up. You must have known who the ruler was as soon as we arrived. It explains why you were so adamant we leave. It also makes clear why you used your Charm."

"I didn't actually lie, I just didn't bring it up."

"A lie of omission, then. It could have been important."

"You think I like talking about all this? Of reminding you how I used to be nothing? I didn't even have a last name. I was property. They didn't call me a slave, but I could still be bought and sold like a pig or cow. I... I was ashamed."

"Alice, I know all this. I paid a hundred gold coins to buy you. Why is it an issue?"

She tugged on her hair more fiercely. "I care what you think about me. I know you know what I am, but I want you to see me as someone special to you."

"Alice," he took hold of both her hands, pulling them free of her hair. "I am going to tell you something very important, and I want you to pay attention to me. All right?"

She nodded silently.

"Growing up, I was taught many sayings to sum up important lessons in a few words. One of the first and most important was this; 'Trust is a dagger pointed at your own heart.' I was brought up to not trust others. I was taught to always expect betrayal."

"How terrible."

He lifted an eyebrow. "Life is cruel, and I learned a great many hard lessons growing up. Every child of every Great House does. Members of my family were dangerous. It was not unusual for them to arrange accidents for one another. Trusting too much or the wrong person would get you killed very quickly."

"I can't believe people in the same family could do that to each other."

"Another of our sayings is, 'Corpses are easy to step over.'"

Alice grimaced in obvious distaste.

"Before setting out on my quest, I trusted only two people; my mother and my sister Gwendolyn. They were the only ones I felt I could put my faith in. Everyone else, every brother, sister, servant, or teacher I expected to betray me. Except for my mother and Gwen, there was no one else I would share a secret with or allow to stand at my back. Do you understand what I am saying? About how precious trust is to me?"

"Yes, I think so."

He leaned forward and placed a slow, soft kiss on her lips.

"I trust you," he whispered.

Her eyes widened. Through the bond, he felt her shock, followed by a wellspring of clear happiness.

"So don't lie or keep secrets from me anymore."

She pressed herself against him. "Yes, darling."

XXX

Lancel was lying in a warm bed, Uma asleep next to him. Her light snoring reminded him of a sickly weasel. She was one of the women he liked to keep on his various estates. Brothels were fun to visit now and again, but he preferred having exclusive lovers. Being discreet with his pleasures was important. After all, one day he would be the Duke of Norwich, one of the most powerful men in all Lothas and an advisor to the king. For a man like him, reputation was everything.

Thoughts about his reputation brought Stratford and Alice back to mind. To think he had almost lain with a monster! To have actually committed bestiality would have ruined him. The king would never allow a man who'd committed such a depravity to be a lord of the realm. So in an odd way, Elsa's greed had saved him. Not that Lancel felt any sort of gratitude towards the fat sow. Her lies had nearly ruined him in the first place. The mere possibility of rumors about him being attracted to a monster made Lancel sick.

Had Stratford been a small village, he and his men would have slaughtered everyone and burned it to the ground. The lives of a few commoners and whores meant nothing compared to his own future. As it was, he could not make an entire city disappear. He'd had to settle for a small lesson and putting some fear into them. If any of those fools talked, he would go back and turn them into dog meat.

Rationally, Lancel was sure everything would be fine. Even if the story spread, who would believe it? Peasants loved to talk about their betters, but their opinions didn't matter. If other lords and ladies heard, they would assume it was idle slander. Every truly great man had enemies, who were always inventing lies. Go to any tavern late at night when tongues were loose, and you would hear how the local lord had fondled a stable boy or slept with a cousin or raped some farmer's pretty daughter. Those sorts of stories were the same wherever you went. They were expected.

So what if the king or his father heard some vague rumor about him and some barmaid who was secretly a monster? What person of importance would take such a thing seriously? Alice was gone, and he would never see or hear from her again. The important thing was the incident would have no effect on his future. He would follow in his father's footsteps and be Duke of Norwich.

Beside him, Uma stirred and her weasly snores continued.

Looking at her, he thought about how common she was, how ordinary. She was a pretty little milk maid from Bristol. He'd decided to make her one of his women. Lancel suddenly wasn't sure why he'd bothered. Uma was enthusiastic and not unskilled with her mouth, but he'd had better.

She lay underneath blankets, but he'd gotten a close look before. Her breasts were barely enough to fill each hand and a bit lopsided. The girl had a slight pot belly small bulges of fat at her hips and thighs. When he bothered to talk to her, she agreed with every word he said and fell over herself to tell him how wonderful he was.

Gods, she was boring.

Alice on the other hand…

Now there was a woman.

Everything about Alice was magnificent, perfect, and unique. The first time he'd seen her, he'd known she'd belong to him. Everything from her hair to her eyes to those ample breasts had caught his attention. When he'd offered to take her to bed, she'd actually defied him! A barmaid in a common whorehouse had refused him. It turned out she was an indentured servant, lower than even an ordinary peasant.

Her refusal had not upset him. Lancel loved a good hunt, and she was clearly a worthy prize. The fact she was a *virgin* made her seem a god's gift. Surely such a woman was meant for a man like him.

The delays while he dealt with that cow Elsa only increased his eagerness. He would dream about Alice, spend the hours on horseback imagining what her kisses tasted like. Thought of undressing her and finally rubbing his face and hands all over those glorious tits. It had been years since he'd wanted anything as much as he'd wanted her. Lancel delighted in the anticipation and in the conquest to come.

Then it all turned out to be for nothing. His angelic beauty was a hideous, inhuman beast. His feelings for her were reduced to a foul jest.

The worst part of it all was he still wanted her, even knowing she was a monster. The thought of forcing her to his will made his manhood start to rise. It would never happen now, but if he could have her but once, in secret, he would.

Then, he would silence her forever.

Lancel shook Uma's shoulder roughly. Thinking of Alice had gotten him too excited to sleep. He would spend a few more days here enjoying himself before it came time to go home.

XXX

It was the second hour, and Celton Poisondagger was at the same place where he had originally met the vampire. Celton's wand was in hand, but he had not cast a spell to provide light. His father had given him strict instructions to draw as little attention as possible. He stood in near total darkness, waiting for the possible arrival of a murderous creature. The thought he might be betrayed and murdered filled his mind. Killing a Poisondagger under such circumstances was most definitely something Lilith would do.

"I take it your father has agreed to my offer?"

The voice from behind made him jump. Not five feet away was Enver. Even being so close, it was hard to make out more than an outline in the darkness. The vampire's fangs were the only part of him Celton could see clearly.

"Where have you been? I came here yesterday and waited for over an hour."

"My apologies." Enver sketched a shallow bow. "You can inform Master Dante my mistress was awake late last night. Obviously, I could not venture out without her being aware of it. I am watched even when I am not watched. Such is the fate of a familiar."

Celton had no idea if it was a lie. "My father is willing to meet with you, but he remains suspicious."

"Hardly surprising. Your father hasn't lived this long by being the trusting sort."

"He wanted me to inform you he will use a Circle of Truth. He plans to interrogate you thoroughly, and if he suspects any sort of deceit will kill you. He and I will be within a protective circle."

"It is to be expected. You Poisondaggers are not known for your courage."

Celton bristled. Unfortunately, such was his family's reputation, but to actually bring it up was rather rude.

"People may mock us, but whenever we walk past, they always watch their backs. We are very good at dealing with enemies in our own particular way. Even your mistress takes care around us."

Enver shrugged. "I suppose."

"In any case, my father is suspicious. He is not the sort to be taken in. Trying to do so is very dangerous."

"Everything about this is dangerous. You can't kill the head of a Great House without taking a risk."

"Quiet!" Celton looked about fearfully, trying to spot anyone who might be lurking in the shadows.

Enver chortled. "Do give me some credit. Unlike you, I can see perfectly in the dark. Rest assured no one else is within earshot."

"Maybe not physically, but there is always scrying magic. My father could be listening to us at this very moment."

"What if he is? I have not said anything he could disagree with. He might take offense at my mention of your family's courage, but I doubt he would call off the meeting."

"You should still be careful."

"I have spent the past seventeen years at Lilith's side. I know how to watch my tongue when I must." There was a sour laugh. "Though I admit to sometimes saying more than I should. Poking at her is one of my few pleasures."

"Saying the wrong word where my father can hear will see you turned to ashes."

"I will keep your warning in mind, Master Poisondagger. Don't be so afraid. I will handle my part. Have you made it clear to Dante no one but the two of you can know about me?"

"Yes, he is aware there are spies in our House. The last thing he wants is to lose a chance to rid himself of his greatest enemy by being careless."

"So long as only the two of you know, everything will be fine."

"If I am able to trust you. You know the old saying."

Enver nodded. "You would be a fool to trust me completely, but you can trust we both want the same thing. Have faith in our common interests rather than in me."

Celton did not like the thought of trusting the vampire even that much, but given what they were trying to accomplish, there was no choice.

"I think my father would be more comfortable if you provided him a sign of your good faith."

"Tell him his head cook Barthel is a Corpselover spy. He has been for at least ten years. Also, there are others. I will be happy to give him the full list when we meet."

"Barthel?" Celton said in disbelief. "He is one of father's favorites! He is one of the most pampered slaves in the castle."

"I am the most indulged servant in Castle Corpselover. Need I say more?"

"No one would have ever suspected him, and you're tossing him away so easily."

Enver waved a hand impatiently. "What do I care? If this pleases your father and eases his mind, it's enough. There are still four other spies, and Barthel doesn't know who they are."

This information would make quite an impression on his father, Celton was sure. Dante would miss Barthel's puddings- they were his favorites. "Let us meet in four days' time at the second hour. There will be an open window on the north side of the main keep. Light will come from it, and it will be marked by golden curtains."

"Please tell your father I look forward to the meeting." In an instant, Enver was gone.

Celton began the long walk home. The upcoming meeting filled him with both hope and dread.

Chapter 16

Wait Your Turn

When she returned from Avalon, Melissa was too exhausted to do much more than eat dinner and go to sleep. Using teleportation twice in one day drained her almost completely of mana. She was not embarrassed as many archmages could only perform it once.

By the following morning, she had fully recovered and set out on the chase. Baron Torrance was kind enough to see her off and mouth some empty words about how he regretted her sudden departure. She was quite sure the baron felt relieved to see her go. Melissa noted Varlos was nowhere to be seen. She would have liked one hour alone with him. She suspected the spymaster knew more about Waldo than she did. Unfortunately, there was no time to track Varlos down.

Minister Barrows had been most generous with his assistance. Not only had she been given gold, a virgin wand, and a new spellbook, the minister had allowed her to set her other tasks aside and pursue Waldo. She had written orders signed and sealed by the minister authorizing her to do *anything* she saw as necessary to deal with Waldo, up to and including giving orders to any other members of the Order she met along the way. Barrows agreed. Finding and dealing with this rogue was the priority. Catching Waldo was now her only concern. Nothing would stand in her way.

The main problem became finding his trail.

She tried scrying magic but to no effect. Melissa was not skilled in it and, despite their run in, lacked a strong personal connection to him. It was also possible he was using protective wards. The next best option was summoning a creature to follow his scent. Unfortunately, summoning monsters was forbidden by the Order. Members were only permitted to summon animals. Summoning a hound or wolf would have helped... if she'd had the necessary talent.

Anyone who could draw mana and cast at least one spell, even if it only levitated a feather, was a mage. Anyone who could use just one of the deeper magics was an archmage. Melissa had a great talent for wind magic and could use many of its most advanced forms. She was even skilled enough use it as a killing force. Not easy to do, as wind was considered the least lethal of the four elements. Outside of wind, invocation was the only other school where she could practice some of the deeper magics. She was competent with many of the basic spells of the other schools, except for summoning, where she had no ability. This was normal. Most archmages could use basic spells of multiple schools, but deeper magics from only one or two. Only Grand Masters could use complex magics from three or more.

Given her lack of options, Melissa needed to go about her search in a more mundane fashion. She would go from village to village asking if anyone had seen Waldo and his companions. Yes, she intended to travel the countryside asking, "Where's Waldo?" over and over. White Mages were memorable, especially travelling with a red haired strumpet and an ogre. It would take time, but once she had his scent, she would track him down no matter where he ran.

Melissa looked at her new wand. She had already carved three words of power into it. The wand worked even better than her old one had. She intended to keep carving words into it to make it a perfectly honed tool.

"*Ventus est fugatus sem.*"

Winds gathered about her and kicked at her heels, launching her into the air. Her breath was sucked out, and she had to gasp in the air as she soared up above the trees.

Flying, it was worth the years of study if only for this. As a rule, she avoided using this spell. It always terrified the ordinary folk to see someone flying through the skies. A large part of her duty was to make the common people accept the Order and see it as their protector and friend. Panicking them was not helpful to such an end.

In this case, Melissa decided it was worth it. A distance taking her a whole day to walk she could cover in less than an hour flying. Melissa could jaunt from village to village until she discovered Waldo.

She was sure it would not take long.

XXX

The sun shone, the sky blazed blue, and there was a gentle breeze blowing- a perfect summer day.

He strolled into one of the countless small villages dotting the local landscape. The place had a name of course, but he didn't know or care what it might be. In his experience, places like this were all the same anyway. The people might complain about some of their neighbors but would still help them in times of trouble. The instinct was always to band together against adversity or any sort of threat from the wider world. They all knew each other, and all lived the same boring lives, year after year, generation after generation. It was a dull existence, but he supposed it was peaceful.

Until it wasn't. Because, soon or late, someone like him always came to places like this, much as wolves were bound to visit any spot where sheep gathered.

He was surprised not to see anyone. Likely, they were all either inside enjoying the midday meal or out working the fields. Even the watchtower was empty. The village was surrounded by a wooden stockade, but its gate was open and unguarded. The villagers must not have been bothered by goblins recently. As he entered, he noticed a couple of dogs. Both of them immediately started barking. Not surprising, he always had that effect on animals.

He took a step in their direction.

One turned and fled. The other lowered his head and let loose a menacing growl.

He took another step closer.

The dog hesitated, let out a whine, and fled.

Smart animals, he thought. Dogs had much better survival instincts than most humans. They didn't try to fight when it was clearly hopeless. Honor, duty, loyalty… empty words meant to convince men to die pointless deaths. Ideals were meaningless. All that mattered was power.

There were sixteen or seventeen thatched huts. All but one was of a basic design. The exception was a cottage made of split logs and connected to a stable, obviously the local inn. He strode to its door and knocked upon it three times.

There was a short pause before a woman's voice spoke. "Who's there?"

"A stranger in need."

Another little wait. The door swung open. A stout woman in an apron stood there. "Welcome to…" She cut off as her eyes widened, and she let out a blood curdling scream. Both hands slammed the door shut again. She was still screaming as he heard what had to be a bar being banged down.

"How utterly rude," Lucius Corpselover said. "Do you always treat visitors so poorly?"

From one of the huts came a man wielding a staff. "What's happened?"

"You wait your turn." The archlich touched thumb to middle finger. "*Xatos ki.*"

The minor spell sent the man flying into the side of his home with enough force to break bones.

Other villagers came out to see what was going on. Lucius had at least a dozen spells able to deal with all of them at once. Simple massacre wasn't his purpose, though. He was here to raise some helpers and to spread a panic. His intent was to kill most of these people and then pay a visit to the local burial ground. Lucius would also make sure to burn everything while he was at it. Pillars of smoke were the fastest and simplest way to tell people at a distance something was wrong. He would allow some to escape. He wanted details to reach Norwich.

A single kick reduced the inn door to kindling.

The woman who had answered and three children cowered in a corner. Their mindless screams and the look of absolute terror on their faces gave him a sense of mild pleasure. He'd forgotten how much fun it was to play with the mundanes.

Lucius crossed the room and began choke the life out of the woman as her children watched.

It really was turning out to be a lovely day.

Chapter 17

Stop Thief

"So what do you think?" Duke Griffinheart asked.

"Ah, it's very nice," Alice said.

"Nice?! You think it's nice?"

"Oh, no, I... I mean it's really something, amazing."

The duke gave a miniscule nod, apparently mollified. "I got it from my grandfather you know."

"Really?"

"He was very proud of it. He would go around showing it off to people."

"Well, who could blame him?"

"You know the muscles in my arm come from spending so much time handling this brute. Yanking it, squeezing it, swinging it around, when I was younger I would spend hours working with it. I would go until my hands bled, and my arms were sore."

"Truly?"

"Yes." He gave a despondent sigh. "Now I'm older, I can't manage such an exertion anymore, but I will still go at it for at least an hour a day."

"Is it really so heavy? I mean, you look so strong and virile, my lord."

As she'd hoped, her words brought a smile.

"Would you like to hold it?"

"Ah, I am not sure. Is it really proper?"

"Merely be careful where you grip."

Alice cautiously approached. "Where do I put my hands?"

"Right here, at the base. Use both and grip it tightly."

She did as she was told. "Like this?"

The duke nodded enthusiastically. "Marvelous. You've held one before?"

"No, this is my first time. I've seen plenty of men with them of course, even a few women."

"Rare, but I've seen it as well. You're a natural. Would you like to try swinging it around a little?"

"Is it safe?"

"So long as you don't let go and don't become too wild, it's fine. You need to get used to the feel of it in your palms. It has a name, you know: 'Lawgiver.'"

Alice gave a slight shake of her head. "Why do men always feel the need to name everything?"

"It's a matter of pride, I suppose. I sometimes use it to punish the wicked. I feel a ruler should handle things personally now and again. I tell you, when they see me holding this in my hand, criminals' knees tremble."

"I believe it." She was already getting used to holding it. It felt surprisingly natural. "If I had one, do you think men would be afraid of me?"

"Likely not at first, but once they saw how you could handle it…"

Waldo entered the dining hall.

"Am I interrupting?"

Alice stood with the duke near the head of the table. In her hands was a broadsword. The blade gave off a minor golden aura. Waldo could sense magic radiating from it, enough to mark a significant enchantment.

"I thought I would show your wife what it feels like to hold a sword. Would you like to try it, Master Rabbit?"

"Not necessary." From one of the hidden pockets of his robe, he produced his wand. "This is all I need."

The duke glanced from the foot-long wand to the four and a half feet of sharpened steel.

"Mine is bigger."

"Mine shoots fire."

Duke Griffinheart considered and gave a grunt. "I can see where that would be useful."

XXX

Waldo, Alice, and Belle were out on the streets of Norwich. Waldo had cast his detection spell, and they walked through the city in hopes of spotting some sign of a monster. But despite his best efforts Waldo had yet to spot anything.

"Well?" Alice asked.

"Nothing," Waldo said. "So far as I can tell, the duke was right. No evidence of monsters inside the city walls."

"Except for us," Belle noted.

"Shush," Alice hissed and glanced up and down the street. No one was particularly close to them. People were still eager to keep their distance.

Belle sent her an eye roll. "Don't be so worried, sweetheart."

"The punishment for a monster being in this city is to be burned at the stake." She turned to Waldo. "So does this mean we can finally leave?"

"Not yet."

"But why not? Everyone we ask says there's nothing to find, and your own magic is telling you the same. Why can't we go?"

"We'll search for at least a couple more days. If we still have nothing then, we can move on."

Alice wanted to be gone from this place now, not in a couple more days. Her only solace was knowing at least they wouldn't be here a week as they had been in Middleton.

"So where do we go when we leave, Master?"

"We'll head north into the marshes."

"What? Darling, that is not a good idea! Have you not been listening to people? The marshes are teeming with goblins. The patrols won't even enter them."

"Which is what makes it an ideal place for a Great Monster. The map I was given told me I'd find one here. But if there isn't one in the city itself, it might be hiding nearby."

Alice was not sure which was worse, going into the marshes or staying here. Thinking about it, she decided a horde of goblins was less frightening than seeing Lancel again.

"You know," Waldo said. "The duke's sword was rather impressive."

Alice immediately narrowed her eyes. "I suppose."

"I've seen a few. My family doesn't specialize in evocation magic, but we did keep some enchanted weapons and armor. The spells usually make the blade's edge sharper and the metal harder. I suspect the duke's sword was given much stronger features."

"I think he said something about being able to cut through trees in one swing."

Waldo nodded. "Some archmage probably spent months working on it, placing exactly the right combination of spells. Every knight, mercenary, and raider dreams of magical arms, but few mages have the necessary skills. The buyers outnumber the sellers at least a thousand to one. I am sure someone would be willing to pay a small fortune for such a sword."

"You really are trying to get us killed, aren't you?"

"Not at all. We can get the sword immediately before we leave."

"Right, we're going to steal the duke's greatest treasure and walk away. How exactly?"

"You owe me five Charms, remember?"

She shut her eyes and put a hand to her face. "Oh, Cannassa have mercy."

XXX

He was trailing them. Having on a faded gray cloak over his worn tunic and trousers, he blended in. No one would think it strange he hung back from a White Mage. Except in times of trouble, folk never wanted them around. He certainly didn't. White Mages were almost as hard on his kind as on monsters. The bastards loved killing criminals and making examples of them. "Such an unreasonable bunch," he muttered beneath his breath.

The authorities here and in most of Lothas were sensible. So long as you didn't steal from a noble or certain important people, the guards didn't get too worked up about a little theft. If you weren't stealing from the wrong persons, the punishment was usually a few lashes in the marketplace. Normally, only novices or incompetents ever got caught. Something which obviously did not apply to him.

Normally, he would have kept well clear of any white. The risk was too great, even for someone as talented as him. But the moment he'd spotted *her* the temptation had been too much to resist. Everyone knew White Mages traveled alone, but this one had arrived with a couple of wenches. One was a woman barbarian, bigger and more muscled than a blacksmith. He wouldn't want to get in an argument with her, never mind anything else. The other traveling companion the wizard had was something entirely different.

He had been with his share of women and then some, but in his life he'd never spotted a beauty like her. Her body was absolutely perfect, with all the right sort of curves in exactly the right places. The face was beautiful, fiery hair caught the eye, and the way her hips swung rhythmically as she walked spoke of grace and elegance.

And those tits! Incredible!

Despite the danger, he'd immediately decided to introduce himself. Most men would think robbing her a poor way to go about it, but in his experience, it always left a strong impression. Women were attracted to men who were dangerous. If you brought them a flower after stealing a purse and begged their forgiveness sounding sincere and such, they would usually not only forgive but spread their legs for you. For a man like him, it was almost unfair.

Of course, before long, most would start to get ideas about love and romance. Even though he was careful never to make those sorts of promises, the girls would still get mad when they found out he was plowing other fields. Women could be so unreasonable about certain things.

Which reminds me, I need to get Marriana some flowers. Benvida, too, and Holli, and is Polla still mad at me? It's been a week. Ah, well, I'll get her flowers, too. I did sleep with her cousin. Most girls don't appreciate that.

Inside his cloak was a single perfect rose. When he saw them turn down Sparrow Way, he waved three fingers over his head. Markus saw and dashed off to set things up. Sparrow Way was a very narrow street, a really big man might be able to touch houses on both sides at once. He picked up his pace to close the distance between him and the most beautiful woman he'd ever seen.

He would grab her by the wrist and twirl her around. In his other hand would be the rose. *For you, my beautiful lady.* Of course she would be taken by surprise and breathless. She would recognize him and probably accuse him of being a thief. *I beg your forgiveness, it wasn't your purse I was after, but your heart.* The ladies always started to melt when they heard the line. Usually, at that moment, he would give them back what he'd stolen. The typical purse only had maybe ten to thirty copper tokes, given how much a pretty Soiled Dove cost, it was a good investment. Unfortunately, he wouldn't be doing it this time. There'd been gold and silver in her purse. More wealth than he would normally see in a whole year. White Mages really were as rich as people said. It would make things harder, but he liked a challenge, and he knew how to win a pretty girl's heart.

As they neared Frog Street, he was within fifteen feet of her. He was careful to keep his head down on the off chance she looked back. Being spotted before he could perform his introduction would ruin the effort. He was close enough to overhear them.

"Why are you so obsessed with us getting gold anyway?" his red haired beauty asked. "I mean, it's not as if you even appreciate it."

How could anyone not appreciate having gold?

"It's necessary for me to bring back proof of my success. Mother would expect sacks of gold along with the skulls of my enemies and slaves. You know, trophies. I don't want to disappoint my mother."

"When exactly did you stop sucking from your mother's teat? The week before we met?"

The white wizard sent her a look of annoyance. He made sure to put a hand over his face until the mage looked away again.

"Which reminds me, we need to start collecting the heads of the people we kill."

"You want us to go around carrying heads?"

"Hmmm," the white wizard said. "We could bring scalps, but skulls are more impressive."

"Don't worry, Master," the muscly savage woman said. "I'll carry them for you."

"Thank you, Belle."

For a moment, the thief considered turning around and walking away. If it was possible this White Mage was even scarier than expected.

But Frog Street was coming up. The wizard and barbarian were walking a little ahead of his beauty. And the red haired woman's tits still drew the eye. Every step she took, every twist of her shoulders or the way the snug blouse accentuated her chest after each ripple of movement drew the eye. The mere thought of getting his hand on her made him salivate. He put two fingers to his mouth and gave two quick whistles.

It looked like Markus had gotten things ready in time. A horse-drawn wagon pulled out and then stopped at the top of the intersection, blocking off Sparrow Way. The White Mage and barbarian had been forced to step lively to keep from being run over. The beauty had been trailing a few steps behind and was momentarily cut off.

"You blind idiot!" she yelled. "You almost ran them over!"

This was the moment. He dashed forward, taking the rose out in his right hand as he deftly grabbed her wrist with his left and yanked, spinning her about. "For you…" was all he was able to get out.

"Eek!"

The girl backhanded him. Despite being just a woman he was sent flying. One moment he'd been about to present her with his flower. The next he was lying on his back in the middle of the street, his pride and rump suddenly aching. He sat up and saw his perfect rose lying atop a dog turd. This wasn't quite going as he'd planned.

"I am so sorry," she approached him. "I don't like being touched by men."

This might not be so bad. He flashed her an embarrassed grin and jumped to his feet. "Then I am sure men from here to the Inner Sea are weeping." Women loved being told how special they were. He expected to get some sort of thanks or nervous denial. Instead, he got a sudden look of recognition and, in his imagination, fangs.

"Hey! I know you! You robbed me."

"True," he stepped back and gave her a practiced bow which seemed at odds with his ragged appearance. "My name is Daring, Cleptus Daring. I am a master thief. But you don't need to be afraid, I..."

"Where is my purse?" Her fists were clenched, and she took a step towards him.

The reaction caught him off guard. It was something he would expect from a man in a bar. Women were always intimidated when they first realized he was an outlaw. This girl seemed to be the exception.

"I am sorry, my sweet, but as you can see, I don't have it with me."

She took another step. Instinctively, he took one back and slid a hand to one of his daggers. He'd been in dozens of fights and barroom brawls in his life, and he could recognize the signs of menace she was sending. He was also painfully aware she was very strong despite being a mere woman. "I want my money back, or I am going to hurt you."

Daring swallowed. He believed her. This was *really* not going the way he'd expected. His gut was telling him it was time to go, but how could he run away from a female? Especially this gorgeous, if scary one?

As he was debating what to do there was a loud creak and some shouts and the whinny of a horse. Daring saw the back of the wagon being lifted about five feet into the air. The homely barbarian girl was holding it up with *one hand.*

"Hey, sweetheart, Master wants to get going."

The decision was suddenly made very easy. Dashing forward, he planted a quick kiss on her lips. It lasted only a fraction of a heartbeat but long enough for him to see her violet eyes widen and to know she tasted as sweet as fresh picked cherries.

"Eek!" She tried to punch him, really punch him, but he was able to duck beneath her fist.

He turned and ran as fast as he could. "I love you!" he called over his shoulder. "Visit the Inn of the Hungry Snake, and we will meet again, my lady."

She rubbed her lips with the back of her hand. "You disgusting pig!"

He laughed. "I've been called worse, my love."

"Come back here! Thief! Stop thief!" She lifted the hem of her skirt and chased him.

"Damn it," he cursed beneath his breath.

The people in his way all stepped aside. The common folk weren't going to get involved. If he ran into some guards on patrol, though, things would get bad.

"I want back what you took from me!"

"You and half the maids in this city." Looking over his shoulder, he was startled to see she was actually catching up. He was fast on his feet and could easily outrun most men. It had been a long while since anyone had threatened to chase him down.

Despite the seriousness of his situation, he couldn't help but gape. Not only were her breasts heaving and bouncing, he was getting a clear view of those shapely legs. Her murderous fury only made her even more irresistible. Scary women had a special sort of allure.

Ahead rested a cart directly below a second story window. Without breaking stride, he ran up onto the cart and leapt off it, stretching to snag the edge of the window sill. He swung his legs and used all of his momentum to fling himself up into the air. He tumbled and landed on his feet atop the tiled roof.

In the street below, he saw his beautiful maid gazing up at him. "I know… I'm amazing."

She was shaking, and he would swear she really did have fangs. "I am going to kill you."

"You will have to get in line, love." He was about to laugh when she ran to the same cart and sprang from it. She missed the window sill… but her fingers clawed into the wooden side of the house with a loud, clear "thunk". She then climbed to the roof like a damn squirrel. His jaw dropped. "I like an aggressive woman, but this is a bit much." He ran again.

She pulled herself onto the roof and pursued him.

"You know I've had women angry with me before. Most usually threaten to send their brothers or husbands after me." He leapt over an alleyway and onto the next building.

"I am getting back my money and then I am going to beat you to death for what you did."

"Do you mean the theft or the kiss?"

"Both!" She leapt over the same alley without hesitation.

"They were both worth it." He ran over the tiles and leapt a second, slightly wider gap. His right foot barely caught the edge and he almost didn't make it across. He kept running but shouted a warning to her. "You need to stop now. You are really putting your life in danger."

She leapt from the edge of the other building and flew through the air as fearlessly as any hawk. Her hands landed and she flipped to her feet. He was gifted with a quick glance of her long, smooth thighs. Then she was running again.

"May Wotal strike me blind! You are a goddess made flesh!"

"Oh, I've heard that before."

She was drawing close. No matter how hard he sprinted she kept with him, and he was starting to tire. "Tell me your name." He felt her grab the back of his cloak.

"It's Alice Rabbit, and I've got you!"

"My heart at least." He slid a dagger into his right palm and cut the draw string about his neck to let her yank the garment off as he kept going.

Caught off guard, she tripped and fell.

When he came to the end of the roof, he saw a street beneath. With no chance of jumping it and too far up to safely leap down, he spotted a rain pipe. As soon as he wrapped his knees and hands about it, there was an ominous creak. He could feel it giving way. With no other choice, Daring slid down it as fast as she could. Halfway to the ground, it snapped off. He let go and tumbled.

The landing was awkward and hard, but he was able to get up. Looking to the rooftop, he saw Alice glowering.

"Come see me at the tavern, love!" He gave her a wave and ran off before she could find a way down.

XXX

There was nothing Alice could do but watch the miserable thief blend into the crowd and get away. She could have caught him easily and hurt him really hurt him… if she could have used her wings. "The tavern of the Hungry Snake," she muttered.

She forced herself to turn and head back. "…the Hungry Snake…"

Schrrrrk. Mortar and rock ground to dust as she passed a chimney. "…Hungry Snake…"

Her talons shaved four uneven, one-inch gouges into the next chimney she walked by. "You want me, Cleptus Daring?" Along with her claws her tail had also come out and was lashing back and forth. "You'll get more of me than you can handle."

XXX

Daring made it back to the tavern with a minor limp and missing his cloak.

"You all right?" Markus asked him.

"Perfectly fine."

Markus noticed him wince as he sat at the bar. "You sure?"

Daring grinned. "Trust me, my friend, a woman like her is worth dying for, never mind a little pain."

Chapter 18

Proper Thanks

The three of them returned to the duke's keep after completing a circuit of the city and finding no signs of either a Great Monster or the thief.

"We should find out where this tavern is and burn the place down."

Waldo gave a weary shake of his head. Alice had gone on and on about her encounter, not only retelling the chase but going into excruciating detail about exactly what she was going to do to this man. "Won't it make it hard to get the purse back if we do that while he is still in it?"

"You're right, darling. I'm letting my feelings get in the way and not thinking this through."

Waldo nodded.

"We go to this tavern, find him, break his legs, make him tell us where the gold is, and then we burn it down with him still inside."

Belle turned to Waldo. "See? Didn't I tell you she was scary?"

"You know, Alice," Waldo said. "There are times when you can be surprisingly cruel."

"I'm a woman."

"Why are you so irate?" Waldo asked. "You weren't this angry when we were actually robbed."

"It's because he deliberately mockd me! He was rubbing what he did in my face and acting as though I were helpless. Not only that he…"

Waldo waited, but she did not continue following her abrupt pause.

"He what?"

Alice wrung her hands and her eyes flickered to the floor. "He… he kissed me."

"Kissed you?" Waldo said in surprise. "You didn't mention it before."

"It's not something I wanted you to know."

"Did you enjoy it?"

"What? Of course not!"

"Pity. Hopefully next time you find someone who knows what they're doing."

Smack!

"Ow!" Waldo rubbed the back of his head. "What was that for?"

"You're unbelievable. Do you care about my feelings at all?"

"Of course I do. Did you not hear me wish for you to have a better experience next time?"

Her eyes bored into him, and if the look were not enough, he could sense annoyance through their bond.

"What? I was being thoughtful!"

Alice opened her mouth to commence yelling at him but felt Belle place a beefy hand on her shoulder.

"Master, I think Alice is upset because you are all right with her being kissed by another man."

"Why wouldn't I be?"

"Because I'm your wife!"

"I know… I know." He sighed wearily. "You keep reminding me. What does marriage have to do with it?"

"A husband is supposed to be upset when another man has intentions towards his wife. You're not supposed to tell me to enjoy it when someone else kisses me."

"Can't I simply see it as him paying you a compliment?

Alice cracked her knuckles.

"Is this like the time we were in Bittford and you were upset because those men were staring, and I didn't mind?"

"Yes! Exactly!"

"Alice, I've already explained my upbringing to you. The castle was filled with sex slaves, and my mother had a string of lovers. Where I come from, men and women are expected to indulge in pleasure whenever they wish."

She turned her hands into fists. "If you ever, 'indulge' with another woman, I will beat you within an inch of your life."

"So it's only all right with men?"

"Yes it is!" Belle said.

"No, it's not! Ewww! How can you even think that? The very idea is a complete abomination!"

"Really?" Belle asked. "You know, sweetheart, the folk around here would say the same about you being with Master."

"That's… that's different."

"You sure?"

Waldo could sense discomfort from Alice and a bit of anger from Gronk.

"I am not interested in men. I simply want to be clear on what the rule is. You have so many of them."

"The rule is simple: once you marry, you should both be faithful."

How limiting. How do they manage not to get bored with each other? "I have said before I don't intend to have sex with anyone I am not married to."

Alice nodded.

Belle appeared downcast. "Really, Master? Not even once? Maybe when you're drunk?"

"I don't think it would be physically possible to get drunk enough. I am sorry, Belle."

Belle scuffed the floor. "You only care about Alice's feelings. Haven't I been a good servant, Master? Haven't I done everything you have asked of me?"

"You have, I have absolutely no complaints and am very glad you belong to me."

"That makes me happy, Master, but you could show me a little consideration from time to time."

"You know, Belle has a point," Alice said. "We are both here for you. We are both ready to follow you anywhere and put our lives at risk. You could be a little more thoughtful. I know you have weird ideas in your head, but if you paid attention you would know what would make us happy."

As a child, he enjoyed treating some of the slaves with kindness. It made him happy to see them happy. He stopped only because Enver killed any servant he was fond of. The vampire wasn't with him anymore. If he wanted to he could reward his servants. "You're right, Alice." The words earned a smile from her. "Wait here. I will be back shortly." Waldo turned to leave.

"Where are you going?"

"To the duke's dungeon." He rounded a corner and was gone. Alice and Belle shared a confused look.

XXX

About a half hour later, Waldo returned. Curled about his right hand was a six foot long, black leather whip. Carried over his left shoulder were rolls of iron chain. "Let's go to your quarters, Belle. We'll do the Clawing Eagle."

Belle's knees almost gave as the ogre swooned from side to side. "Really, Master?"

"Yes, you saved my life, and I never gave you proper thanks." He let the whip uncurl and drew back his arm and swung it forward. The whip sliced the air with a loud, audible snap. "Now come along... you've been bad."

"Yes, Master!" Belle followed on his heels like a puppy.

Alice stood rooted to the spot and watched them go with her mouth hanging open. "This isn't what I meant."

XXX

Lothasians buried their dead.

The fact was a great boon to Lucius Corpselover. After he slaughtered and reanimated the residents of a village, he visited the local cemetery. Each time, he left he had more obedient followers shuffling along behind him. Having already visited three villages, Lucius deliberately allowed a few survivors to escape from each to allow word to spread of what was happening. It surprised him when it wasn't until he approached village number four opposition at last appeared.

Twelve soldiers on horseback led by a knight were drawn up across the road. Behind them was a knot of perhaps thirty men armed mostly with bows, spears, and pikes. A few of them had leather jerkins. The rest wore simple field clothes. The men on foot were obviously locals defending their homes, boys barely in their teens mixed with gray-haired grandfathers. At the gate of the village were all the women and children with bundles on their backs and cloth sacks in their hands. They were ready to flee, but waited to see if these brave heroes could save them.

It had to be hard, standing outside their village watching an archlich and hundreds of skeletons and walking corpses come down the road. Of course, if they'd possessed the sense the Dark Powers gave a house cat, all of them would have fled by now.

The men on horseback had trouble controlling their mounts. The animals neighed and refused to stay still, while their riders struggled to keep them in place. It was more evidence proving animals had the better survival instinct.

The knight drew his broadsword and stood up in his stirrups. He probably thought it made him seem imposing. "I am Sir Preston of Tiverton. In the name of Duke Theos Griffinheart of Norwich, servant to his majesty King Leo Coramoor, Holder of the Keys, Guardian of the Pass, Protector of the Land and Realm of Lothas, I command you and your foul minions to depart."

Lucius came to a halt. His mindless servants did the same. "I see. Then I will go. Please give my apologies to your duke and king." Lucius bowed low.

The young knight's mouth opened and closed wordlessly. "Truly? You will leave us in peace?"

Lucius held out his wand. It was made of human bone, and six words were carved into it: Corpselover, pride, power, Tyver, Kara, and Walter. "Clearly, you don't appreciate my sense of humor. *Fulmina ictas ivaros est domina sagittal norum aliz.*"

Above and around him over a hundred bolts of energy came into existence. Each one was the size of an iron nail and crackled with power. With a flick of his wrist, he fired them off. None of the horsemen had magical armor or protective wards and so were completely vulnerable to magical attack.

One of the bolts struck Sir Preston in his left eye and burned a hole through to the back of his head. Three other bolts struck his armor and melted it to burn the doublet underneath and scar his skin, but did not have the energy to penetrate further. The other soldiers on horseback all wore chainmail. The bolts went through them as though they were made of straw. In an instant, the air was filled with the smell of blood, melted iron, and seared meat. Screams came from both men and women as eleven bodies toppled lifelessly from saddles. Eleven horses hurtled in every direction.

By a seeming miracle, one rider remained alive and completely untouched.

"Horseman," Lucius called out. "Hurry back to your duke and give him this message. Tell him to send out Waldo Rabbit and his companions to face me. If your heroic White Mage does not come out, I will lay waste to Norwich as I have the places I have visited. Now, go!"

The soldier brought his terrified mount under control and then galloped away as quickly as he could. When Lucius turned attention back to the locals, he was not surprised to see the militia had dropped most of their weapons and run. They were helping the women and children get away as quickly as possible.

Lucius could have cut them down like ripe wheat but decided not to bother. The more who escaped, the quicker the panic would spread. He began walking again, and his undead followed after. He needed to burn down the village and fields, clear out the local cemetery, and then it was on to the next village.

Chapter 19

Time To Go

Waldo finished carving the last letter and blew to clear away the shavings and dust. Four words of power were now carved into his wand: Lilith, Gwendolyn, Alice, and Gronk. He put the dagger away into the sheath strapped to his forearm. Waldo grimaced as he rolled his right shoulder. "My arm is still sore from yesterday. I never realized how tiring it is using a whip."

"Really don't want to hear any more about that, darling."

They were alone in their quarters after another fruitless tour of the city. Alice glanced at his wand. "When you find your third monster will you add its name, too?"

"Most likely."

"Oh."

He peered at her. There was disappointment coming through the bond. "Something wrong?"

"No, it's only I feel a little less special to you."

"Want me to service you?" He knew immediately it was the wrong thing to say. Not only did she glare at him, he sensed anger replace disappointment.

"What did I say yesterday about paying attention and understanding what matters to people?"

"What? I listened. Why do you think my arm is sore?"

Alice blew out a frustrated breath. "Never mind. Since we found out where the Hungry Snake is, can we go there and teach Cleptus a very slow and painful lesson?"

Waldo nodded. "When we are ready to leave. After all, he stole from me as well. Not punishing him would set a bad precedent."

"When can we go? We've been all over this place, and you say there's no sign of any monsters. Can't we depart now?"

"I want to do one more search to be certain. If we find nothing tomorrow, we can leave the following day."

"So we have to be here two more days?"

Waldo was going to answer when he noted quite a lot of commotion coming from outside their quarters, followed almost immediately by a loud rap at the door.

"Is it dinner time already?"

Opening the door, he found a knight along with five guards. All six men looked grim. "The duke wishes to speak with you, Master Rabbit. Come with us."

The knight did not sound particularly deferential and had a hand resting on the hilt of his blade.

XXX

Waldo expected to be brought to the dining hall. Instead he was escorted to a cramped study he hadn't visited before. Inside were the duke and three other men, all of them soldiers. They hovered over a small table covered in maps. His arrival was met by frowns and an unpleasant silence. The knight who had escorted him entered the room as well. The door slammed shut behind him.

The mood reminded him of his mother dealing with a family member who had done something stupid. As he had often been on the receiving end of such meetings, he knew they were never pleasant. "You wanted to see me, Duke Griffinheart?"

The duke's usual friendly mood was missing. "Tell me, Master Rabbit, what sort of horror have you brought to my lands?"

"If you're referring to Belle, I have to say that's a bit harsh."

"Don't play stupid games with me," the duke growled. "I have had hundreds of refugees flooding through my gate with tales of horror about a horde of undead. They are led by one with glowing eyes and black robes, a lich. One of my own soldiers rode in to tell me the thing mentioned you by name."

Well that explains the bad mood. "I am not surprised. I have a fearsome reputation. Undead everywhere are terrified of The Rabbit. I am sure the forces of darkness rose up the moment they learned I was near."

"You have brought destruction and ruin to the people under my protection."

"We White Mages do what we feel necesary. Did I mention we are plotting to take over the world?"

The soldiers in the room muttered and placed hands on the hilts of their swords. The duke pressed both palms on the table. "Some people do say such things, though I have never heard those words from a White Mage."

"I like to be forthright."

"Many of noble blood distrust your order, but I am sure you know this to be true. You can hardly blame us given how… zealous some of your compatriots can be."

Waldo nodded. "We are definitely a dangerous lot and not to be trusted."

The duke and his men shared an uneasy look. "Be that as it may, I have always had respect for you White Mages. Especially due to your attitude towards monsters. I agree completely they should be exterminated, not allowed to infest parts of the world until they overbreed and go out to murder decent folk."

"Very enlightened of you."

"The goblins are a problem we have always had to deal with and one we know how to handle. Before you came here these lands had never been plagued by undead. Tell me, did you know you would bring them to my doorstep?"

Waldo gave an uneasy smile. "What are you suggesting? I have undead chasing after me wherever I go? Quite a silly notion don't you think?"

The duke looked at him intently. Waldo was all too aware he was not a very good liar.

"Perhaps you did not deliberately summon them, but the fact is the foul creature which leads them named you. It demanded you and your women be sent out to it. You cannot deny a connection."

"As I said, I have a fearful reputation among evil creatures. I am sure many want to destroy me."

"Perhaps," the duke let one beefy finger tap repeatedly. "Whatever the cause, I mean to deal with this threat. Come the morning, I am riding out with my entire garrison. You will be at my side, Master Rabbit. I expect you to use your full power to aid me."

Waldo gave him a wide smile. He prayed to the Dark Powers it looked convincing. "Naturally. Being a White Mage what would I rather do than face the undead?"

The duke's head bobbed. "It should be a glorious battle. Please eat a hearty meal and get a good night's sleep. It may take a day or two for us to locate the enemy, and I want you at your peak. Your companions will remain here. I have no idea what the custom is in the Misty Isle, but here we don't take women into battle."

"I am grateful for your concern."

"You can go now."

The knight who had escorted him opened the door, and Waldo found himself being dismissed like one of the duke's footmen."

As soon as Waldo was gone, Sir Berrs spoke in a low voice.

"Arrogant, isn't he? 'We're plotting to take over the world. We're a dangerous lot and not to be trusted.' He might as well have been openly threatening you." Berrs tightened his grip on his sword.

"He was lying," the guard captain stated. "He knows more about this than he pretends."

"Yes, obviously," the duke said. "No white travelling abroad would be so poorly trained in hiding his thoughts. It was a message."

"You should have called him on it, my lord," the captain said.

"It would be dangerous, perhaps more dangerous than ten times these undead. The White Mages are playing some sort of game with us. Never doubt it."

"It is most wise to keep his women here as hostages."

"Guests," the duke rumbled. "Never hostages. Hopefully, we will go out, and Master Rabbit will show me some of this fearsome power he claims to have. With luck, we will find this scourge and wipe them out before they can cause any further harm."

"What of the harm they have already done?" Sir Berrs asked. "All of the people already killed and villages burned. If the whites caused all this merely to put on a demonstration we should…"

"What?" the duke asked coldly. "Openly accuse him? Have a trial and give him a taste of Lawgiver?"

"I have heard suggestions I have liked less."

"No. There will be no accusations, no arrests, and no accidents. I will send a message to King Leo with my suspicions, but nothing more. Whatever I may believe, the whites are much too powerful to openly oppose. We will watch him carefully and play the game, as well."

Sir Berrs lowered his head. "As you say, my lord."

When Waldo returned, he knocked on Belle's door, and both of them joined Alice. "Change of plans," Waldo told them. "We are leaving tonight."

Chapter 20

The Hungry Snake

It was well past dinner time when the duke at last emerged from the meeting and headed back to his quarters. The situation was horrible. Not only because so many good people had died, but also due to the strong possibility it was all some Avalon plot. When he and his troops dealt with these undead horrors, some of his men were bound to be killed. Even if Master Rabbit proved to be as skilled as he claimed, there would be casualties. The soldier who'd brought in the report had witnessed hundreds of these creatures following their master. The villagers who had come seeking shelter claimed the entire countryside was infested with thousands upon thousands of them, but he knew better than to listen to frightened peasants. Fighting against hundreds meant a pitched battle, and you could not win a battle without taking some losses.

All of the possible consequences were terrible to be sure, yet Theos had a spring to his step and a smile on his face. He could not deny he was looking forward to leading out his soldiers come the morning. The thought of battle, glorious bloody battle, excited him. He'd fought in six campaigns against the goblins. As a knight, he'd led countless patrols and gone questing to foreign countries. The years and the pounds had accumulated, but at heart he would always be a warrior. Theos had no idea how many more years he had left. How many more times would he still be able to ride in the saddle and lead men with his sword in hand? And this was no ordinary patrol or clash with marauding goblins. Destiny now led them to fight the forces of true evil. Songs of tribute were sure to follow, while the people spoke of it for generations to come. His name would ring the longest and loudest.

So while he deplored the needless death and destruction and loathed the idea he was being used in some sort of plot, Theos could not pretend to being unhappy. As he approached his quarters he spotted something that made him happier yet.

"Duke Griffinheart, I pray I am not disturbing you." The beautiful Alice performed a curtsey for him, giving a splendid view of her bosom.

Theos felt the blood rushing to a certain part of his anatomy. He hadn't been able to take his eyes from this lovely woman since her arrival. It was obvious why his son had been obsessed with her. Had she not already been married, he would have gotten her into his bed. "You could never disturb me sweet lady. Tell me what brings you here?"

He could see her arms shaking slightly. She hesitated to answer. Could Master Rabbit possibly have sent her to him as an appeasement? Men of significance sometimes did that sort of thing. A beautiful woman made for an excellent peace offering. A mistress would make a discreet visit and depart before the sunrise. How better for important men to smooth over a difference?

Such was reserved for common women who didn't matter. You never offered a wife. Though who knew what a White Mage might do? Everyone said they would do anything to get what they wanted. If this were the case, Theos would not refuse and be rude. *He is a foreigner, and a white. It's not surprising if he is a bit uncivilized.*

At last Alice looked up into his eyes. Her exotic pale violet orbs filled his vision. He felt himself getting light headed and licked his lips. The feeling reminded him of being a youth again. He was losing himself in those wondrous eyes. "My lord, it embarrasses me to say this, but there is a request I wish to make."

"Please ask. More than anything I should wish to please you."

"Oh, such a relief. In that case, my lord, would you give it to me?"

His smile was so wide and eager he thought his face might split. "Yes! Of course! As much as you want!"

"Truly? You don't mind? I know it's asking a great deal and a huge imposition, but if you would let me hold it in my hands, I know it would give me comfort and help me sleep tonight."

"Don't let my age fool you. I expect you won't get much sleep."

Alice raised an eyebrow. "What does your age have to do with it?"

He nodded. "Exactly."

She appeared a bit unsure. "If you are certain, could you give it to me?" She held out both hands.

"You mean here? In the hall?" There were a couple of his guards standing not twenty feet away watching.

"Is there a problem, my lord?"

What a bold and shameless woman! How had Lancel not bedded her? "I would much prefer we do this within my rooms where no one can see."

"I am not sure I understand, my lord. What difference does it make whether you give me your sword here or in your quarters?"

"My sword?" he asked in confusion.

She nodded. "You said you would give it to me."

"You were asking about my sword? But... but I thought..."

She clasped both hands together.

"You're not changing your mind, are you, my lord? I know it is a bother, but the feel of your mighty blade in my hands would help comfort my troubled mind. I remember the power of it. Nothing else could compare. Please, allow me to keep it for just one night?"

She was staring at him with those eyes of hers.

XXX

Lying in bed, the duke couldn't quite believe he had actually agreed. He would sooner give up an arm than his family blade. But staring into her eyes, he hadn't been able to tell her no.

He would get the sword back from her before setting out. It didn't make any real difference.

XXX

When Alice returned, she held the sheathed blade in front of her with both hands. On the scabbard was the image of a griffin in flight with an exposed heart, all of it in golden thread.

"Good," Waldo said. "Everything is loaded on Gronk's back, and we are about ready to leave."

"You know, Master, I think you want me more as a pack mule than anything else." The ogre was still disguised as a beefy human female, who now looked to have a tent and two very stuffed backpacks piled atop her back.

"Don't be silly. I value you for your ability to kill things. Your carrying heavy loads is a bonus."

"I am going to say this just one more time." Alice handed the sword to Waldo. "This is a really, really, *really* bad idea. Stealing Lawgiver is guaranteed to make us the duke's mortal enemies."

"Rabbit Slayer." Waldo handed the sword to Gronk.

"Excuse me?"

"Until we sell it, I've decided to give the sword a new name, an alias if you will, to help hide its origins."

"And the name you came up with is 'Rabbit Slayer'?"

"What? Is there another famous weapon with the same name?"

Alice gave a weary shake of her head. "It's not even worth it," she muttered. "Anyway, I used one of my Charms like you asked. So you have four left."

He nodded. "There is nothing to worry about. We are quitting Norwich, and as soon as we finish searching the local area, we are leaving Lothas behind."

"I'm not sorry to be going, but how exactly do we leave? The only gate shut at sunset."

"You can fly me over the wall and away from here. Once we land, I can summon Gronk to me since he's my familiar."

"Wait a minute. You want me to fly us out? Uh, darling, you do realize there's a full moon tonight and the guards have bows and arrows, don't you? What do you suppose they'll do when they spot a succubus going past with a mage in her arms?"

"I expect you can soar by and be out of range before they can even react."

Alice rolled her eyes. "I only soar when I am solo. When I am carrying you, I have all the grace of a three legged sow. We'll be a very big, very slow moving target. Gronk may be able to shrug off arrows, but you and I are going to end up like the straw targets."

"It's a risk I am willing to take." Waldo thought for a moment. "Maybe it would help if you lost a little weight."

Alice's eyes narrowed and he felt of spike of anger. "I could drop you while we're in the air."

"Why are you being so hostile? It's a reasonable suggestion. I've seen your thighs."

"What?"

"Master." Belle had finished tying the sword onto one leg and placed a hand on Waldo's shoulder. "Do you know what a badger is?"

"Some sort of woodland creature I believe."

"Yes, furry, short legs, pointy head, kind of tasty. They're not much to look at, but if you bother them, they can turn nasty. Even bears tend to avoid badgers. If a person were to start poking at one he might lose a finger for his trouble."

"All right. I am not sure why you are telling me this. Are there a lot of them in the marshes?"

Belle nodded in Alice's direction. "You're poking the badger right now, Master, and from the way she is looking at you, I think you might lose something a lot more precious than a finger."

"All I said was she could stand to lose some…"

"Poking!" Belle stuck a beefy finger in Waldo's ribs. "We girls are sensitive about our figures."

Waldo rubbed his side. "You do recall the way you look right now is only an illusion."

"I mean in spirit."

"Anyway," Alice ground out. "My point is trying to fly you over the city wall is not a great plan."

"Since the gate is shut, it is our only option."

"Why are we doing this again?" Belle asked.

"Because if we don't leave tonight, I am going to end up facing my grandfather, the archlich."

"Didn't you already beat him, Master?"

"No, I survived, barely, and only because it didn't take me seriously. We are in entirely different leagues. If I faced my grandfather again, I would have no chance."

Alice nodded her agreement.

"So, let's be off."

"We are visiting the Hungry Snake before we leave, though." Alice was opening and closing her hand.

"Yes, Alice."

XXX

The three of them headed out, only to find a pair of guards at the stairwell.

"Are you going somewhere, Master Rabbit?"

"Ah, my companions and I wanted to go for a short stroll before I set off in the morning."

"I am sorry, but none of you are to leave the keep. The duke's orders," one of the soldiers said.

"It's for your own safety," the other one hastened to add.

"I am glad Duke Griffinheart is so worried about us."

"Is that Lawgiver?"

Waldo sighed. Alice and Gronk could easily deal with these two, but he didn't want to set off an alarm. They needed to sneak away quietly.

"Alice, why don't you use one of your Charms and solve this?"

She crossed her arms over her chest. "What do you mean one? I see two men standing here."

"Oh, come now. This should count as one use."

"It's two or nothing."

"You're being unreasonable."

"Call it revenge for the thighs."

"Badger." Belle poked a single finger in his direction.

The two soldiers eyed one another. "Perhaps we should go and speak to the duke."

"Fine," Waldo grumbled. "It'll count as two."

Nodding, Alice stepped forward and looked into the eyes of the guards.

XXX

Outside the keep's gate, a full squad of soldiers led by a sergeant halted them.

"I am sorry, Master Rabbit, but you and your companions are not permitted to leave."

Waldo glanced at Alice. "I don't supposed…"

"I count eight men, you're going to be deep in my debt."

"Oh, come on!"

"Pardon me, Master Rabbit, but is your savage carrying Lawgiver?"

Waldo groaned and wondered if it would be easier to tell Belle to start smashing.

XXX

In the end, Alice agreed to only count two Charms against the soldiers at the gate. It still meant all the Charms he had earned were now spent. They were able to leave without any alarm being raised. As they made their way through the poor quarter of town, Waldo was not happy.

"Everyone keeps noticing the sword, Master. You sure wearing it is such a good idea?"

"My grandfather, a Great Monster, and who knows what else may be in the area. Since we have a magic sword, we may as well keep it within reach." He glanced at Alice. "If we need to get information, don't expect me to ask you to use your ability again."

They approached an old building bursting with the sounds of laughter and loud talk. Outside the door hung a wooden sign with a serpent devouring its own tail.

Alice smiled. Her fingers flexed at the side of her skirt as she stared at their destination with a strange longing. "Don't worry, darling. This is one time I really don't want to do things the easy way."

Chapter 21

A Most Excellent Thief

The light of several torches bathed the inside of the tavern. The air thickened with smoke, not only from burning rags on sticks but from smoldering tobacco pipes. Underneath lay the scents of cheap ale, sweat, and vomit. About fifty men packed the small common room, not a woman to be seen. In one corner, four burly patrons put down copper coins and tossed dice. At the bar and at the tables, men drank from large mugs filled with ale the color of mud. They argued and told stories, laughed and called each other liars. At one table, two fellows played cups for thirty copper traks stacked in neat, separate piles. Several crowded around watching, ready to shout at the first sign of cheating.

Most customers in worn and faded clothing had callused hands with thick, dirtied nails. Many had greasy hair and unkempt beards. Scars seemed common, and a few missed an ear or finger. Not a place for women or for gentle folk, the Hungry Snake made a refuge for a rough element, a safe place where they could gather and enjoy a respite before getting ready for another hard day.

So when the door opened and Alice stepped inside, it was clear she was out of place. Every eye drew to her, and all laughter and conversation died away. Even those playing dice or cups stopped so they could stare. Head held high and back straight, she sauntered slowly to the bar. Every step caused her hips to roll. Mouths hung open as the customers were unable to look away for even an instant.

So focused on her were the men, no one seemed to even notice the arrival of two strangers a moment after.

Alice pretended not to notice all the hungry stares and the way some mouths drooled. It was easy enough. She didn't have to acknowledge them to know they were drowning in lust. Alice wouldn't be hungry for at least a week. When she reached the bar, she put her back to it and at last looked over her audience. "I am looking for a man named Cleptus. He stole something of mine, and I want it back."

A voice from the crowd rang out. "If it's your virginity, I doubt you'll be getting it back. Trust me. You ain't the first to ask."

Ripples of laughter cascaded through the room. It didn't particularly bother her. All the years as a barmaid had taught her how to ignore rude men. "What he stole wasn't nearly so precious." Her reply produced a moment of surprised silence, followed by even more laughter.

"Well that's true," a man's voice replied when the laughter had quieted. "Even though it was a small fortune, I don't doubt your first would be a treasure beyond counting." From one of the tables he stood and began to stroll towards her.

Alice recognized him and her eyes narrowed. "You have a sweet tongue… for a thief."

"Oh, the ladies all say they like my tongue. They like other parts even better."

His banter produced howls.

"What you stole from me would be enough to buy all your pieces a thousand times over. No matter how glib you may seem, you're nothing but a common thief."

"Oh, love, you wound me. It's not so at all."

She lifted one eyebrow. "You're pretending not to be a thief?"

"What I am saying is I am the legendary Daring. A man who has never been caught, who can pick any lock and move silently through the night without any trace. I, lovely lady, am a most excellent thief." He stood before her and bowed with a flourish.

She waited until he had finished and then grabbed him about the neck with one hand and slammed him into the bar. "I am one really angry woman. Which of us do you think is the more dangerous?"

Her answer produced the loudest hilarity yet. He tried to remove her grip but to no effect. He remained pinned against the bar. No one got up to try and help Cleptus. They remained where they were enjoying the show. Seeing his face turn red, Alice loosened her hold enough for him to breathe.

"You know, you really are a strong wench. What's your secret?"

"I am a goddess made flesh, remember?"

"You are indeed, my love. What say we sit down somewhere and talk this out? We can go somewhere nice and quiet."

"There's nothing for us to talk about. All I want from you is my purse."

"I've already told you, my beautiful red haired enchantress, I can't give you back your coins."

"Maybe you'll feel different after I've hurt you."

"You know, you're not the first woman to feel anger towards me. Though usually it comes after we've gotten to know each other." Unnoticed by her, he tapped the fingers of his left hand on the bar three times in quick succession. "Most women settle for slapping me. Grabbing me by the neck, though. How rough, how unladylike. What other sorts of things do you do, love?"

From one of the tables two brawny fellows stood. One had a wooden club in his hand, the other a length of rope. They walked behind Alice. No one gave any sort of warning of what was about to happen. Before they could reach her, a six-foot tall stranger stepped in their way. He was a plain looking man who spoke with a lisp. "You need to let a girl handle her problems in her own way." Snatching hold of both fellows, he casually tossed them clear across the room hard enough to knock them out.

This suddenly brought everyone to their feet, knives were produced in many hands. The mood changed from jovial to hostile in the blink of an eye.

"*Pyro.*" From a different stranger, a stream of fire flashed overhead. It struck a wooden beam and set it alight. Fortunately, some of the people near it were able to douse the flames before they spread.

"A wizard!" someone cried. "It's a damn wizard!" Men staggered back. Those near the door fled.

"Careful! You want to burn this place down?" the bartender shouted.

"It would likely be a small loss," the ordinary looking man said, his wand at the ready.

The tavern's customers kept their distance. They were the sort to welcome a fight, but facing down a magic user was something else entirely.

"Your friends look different from the last time I saw them," Cleptus said.

"I know. My husband's magic is amazing."

"My invitation was only for you."

"I would have thought from our first run-in, it was clear I wasn't interested in you. I simply want my purse back."

"So it's all about the money? What a shame." His left hand tapped the bar twice, paused, and tapped it twice more. "I certainly don't want to have a White Mage angry with me."

Alice narrowed her eyes and tightened her grip. "So now you're going to be reasonable?"

"Hey, I'm no hero. I know when it's time to quit."

"I don't trust you."

"Not surprising, I did rob you."

"Alice," the disguised Waldo said. "Time is pressing."

"Fine. Gronk, give me some rope so I can tie his hands."

XXX

"You know, you're much too good at tying a man up. It's not your first time is it?"

"Shut up." Alice gave him a shove to keep him walking.

"Trussing a great thief like me this way is a bit insulting."

Daring had his wrists bound tight and was leading them to the back of the tavern. As soon as they exited the common room many of the customers fled.

"I'm sure the three of us will be able to handle you. You know, if this is some sort of trick, I am going to take it out of your hide."

"Has anyone ever told you for such a lovely lady you have a really violent disposition?"

"Only with you. I happen to be very sweet and gentle with everyone else."

"Actually…" Waldo began.

Alice flashed him a look that *dared* him to say one more word.

"Never mind."

Daring chuckled as he brought them to an unlocked door. "Grab a torch." With bound hands he opened it to reveal a simple closet. There were mops, buckets, piles of dirty rags, bowls, and chipped mugs.

"You hid my purse in here?" Alice asked in disbelief.

Reaching in he pulled a switch concealed beneath one of the shelves. There was a click. Daring pushed the back of the closet to reveal it was a hidden door. Behind it was a ladder leading down into darkness.

"Not exactly."

XXX

They soon found themselves in a damp tunnel with a single torch to provide light.

"These are the sewers," Daring said. "They run all under Norwich. My friends and I added secret entrances and rooms. We can go from one end of the city to the other in complete secrecy and disappear after a job." He turned to Alice. "Impressed?"

"I'm standing ankle deep in shit trying not to throw up, and you expect me to be impressed?"

"You have no idea how much work it took to add all these entrances and rooms without anyone finding out." He actually sounded hurt.

"Brag about it to an engineer then, Cleptus."

"Actually, love, I always just go by my last name. Daring suits me better."

"Be glad I'm even addressing you by name, Cleptus. I should call you thief."

"It's Daring."

"Cleptus."

"Daring."

"Cleptus."

"Daring."

"Cleptus."

"This seems oddly familiar," Waldo said.

"Want me to knock their heads together, Master?"

"Sure."

Alice sent her husband a hooded look. It did bring the argument to a halt.

"You really should be more awestruck," Cleptus said. "We can even get outside the city without being spotted. Makes it real easy to smuggle things."

Waldo, Alice, and Gronk all suddenly focused on him. "Wait a minute. You have a way to get out of Norwich in secret?" Waldo asked.

"I just said that didn't I?"

"This is perfect. After we recover our coins, you can lead us from the city." Waldo's companions both nodded.

Cleptus wore an amused smirk. "And why does a White Mage need to sneak away in the middle of the night? Don't your sort come and go as you please?"

"It doesn't matter."

"Why should I help you?" Cleptus asked. "These sewers run for miles, and the tunnels all look alike. It's real easy to get lost down here. If you do stumble over an exit, there's nothing to say it won't be right in front of a guardhouse. Why should I do you any favors?"

Alice leaned in close, baring fangs not there a moment before. "Because we will kill you if you don't."

Without warning, he stepped forward and delivered a sudden, rough kiss on her lips.

Alice's eyes widened and she instinctively shoved him as hard as she could, knocking him on his ass five feet from her. "Eek!"

Despite now lying in sewer water, Cleptus gave a hearty laugh as he slowly sat up. "For such an aggressive woman, you're actually pretty modest in some ways. What would happen if I did something more than kiss you?"

"I'd rip you in half," she growled and took a couple of steps towards him.

Waldo put himself in her way. "Alice, we need him, remember?"

She redirected her anger at her husband. "Is that all you have to say? Another man kissed me right in front of you."

"Fine, I promise to give him a whipping as soon as we don't need him anymore." He turned to look at the thief. "You don't enjoy it, do you?"

Cleptus stared up at Waldo open mouthed. Gronk reached down and yanked the thief to his feet. "Don't worry. Master is real good at whippings."

"You're not a very friendly bunch, are you? Being a little more pleasant might help as we negotiate."

"You're my prisoner. Why do you think I need to bargain with you?"

"Same reason why anyone ever does. I have something you want, and you have something I want."

"You mean like your life and limbs?"

"I was thinking of the gold. What do you say about forgetting about your coins, and I show you the way out of the city instead? We can call the contents of your purse the fee for my services."

"You are not in a position to bargain with me, thief."

"Are you sure about that? I know these tunnels. I can keep you going in circles for days if I like."

"With you at our side the entire time."

"Assuming you can hold me. I am a most excellent thief."

"You got captured pretty easy for a great thief," Alice pointed out.

"Catching is one thing, holding another."

"I am not going to negotiate with you," Waldo said.

"Then good luck finding your coins *or* a way out."

"You know, thief, I've seen prisoners before. They usually beg for the chance to save themselves. They don't normally try and make demands."

"I'm not some helpless captive in a cell." He looked about. "We are all in the same situation, and right now you need me more than I need you. So if you're smart, you'll make a deal with me."

Waldo stood there in silence for a moment. "You don't think I can compel you to do what I want?"

"Not easily. I'm a stubborn cuss."

"I can think of a way to get your obedience."

"I am not Charming him," Alice said.

"Not what I had in mind. Gronk, you can eat one of his fingers, one of the small ones."

"Really, Master?"

"Sure."

Gronk grabbed Daring's left hand and brought it to his mouth.

"Now, will you agree to help me? Or do I tell Gronk to go ahead."

Cleptus grinned. "This isn't a very good bluff. Obviously you would never…"

"Do it, Gronk."

Chomp!

"Aaaaahhhhhh!"

As Cleptus clutched at the bleeding nub, Waldo spoke. "One of the many lessons my mother taught me was to never bluff when you make a threat."

Coming to an intersection in the tunnels, they saw the image of a chicken scrawled on the tunnel wall. "We turn right here."

Cleptus was led the way with Waldo right behind. Then came Gronk holding the torch, and finally Alice brought up the rear. Going down the new tunnel there was the image of a cat.

"Why do you use animals to mark your tunnels?" Waldo asked.

"Not all of us can read, my lord wizard," Cleptus sneered.

"My proper title would be Master Rabbit. You don't like me very much do you?"

Cleptus held up his bound wrists. On his left hand was a thumb and three fingers. "Does my dislike surprise you?"

"I healed your wound. Otherwise, it would have definitely become infected."

"You expect me to be grateful? I had my pinky bitten off!"

"You know, where I come from merely speaking to me with such a tone would get you your tongue ripped out, if you were lucky. Never mind the fact you stole from me."

"Let me guess. Stealing is punishable by death."

Waldo nodded. "Usually by beheading, though impalement is also an option. Depending when you are caught, you might also be forced to fight to the death. You should be thankful I still intend to let you live once you've helped me."

"I don't believe you. Everyone knows White Mages are as hard on criminals as they are on monsters."

"You might be surprised. My attitudes are a bit more liberal than my brethren."

Cleptus gave a snort and rubbed his wound. "Yes, you are an angel of mercy."

"Being insulting is not going to help you. You stole from me, and I am within my rights to do as I please with you, but I am willing to spare you so long as you help me."

"And I'm supposed to believe you?"

"Of course. I'm a White Mage. Doesn't everyone say we're trustworthy?"

"You don't want to know some of the stories they tell about your kind." Cleptus shook his head. "Markus and the others were right. I should have stayed away from you and your friends."

"Why didn't you?"

"Obviously, I was blinded by your wife's beauty. I fell in love at first glance, curse my romantic nature."

"As if your sort would even know what love is," Alice said.

He smiled back at her. "Now there you're wrong. I can love quite well, if not always wisely."

"I've known men like you all my life. You only ever love with your eyes, never with your hearts."

"Unlike your husband, I suppose? He loves you with his whole heart?"

Alice opened her mouth to answer yes, but she hesitated. That Waldo genuinely cared about her she didn't doubt. Unlike every other man she'd ever met, she knew his feelings were more than simple lust. But did he love her with his whole heart? He'd made the point of telling her he trusted her. The declaration made her happy, but trust wasn't actually the same as love, was it? What did his feelings for her really come to? He certainly didn't act like a normal husband. Most men wouldn't offer to trade their wives for five sheets of velum, not even as a joke.

Yet he had put his life in danger to save hers. He'd healed her and protected her, apologized for hurting her. He'd taken her virginity and given her the most soul shattering pleasure. And even if it had been for his own reasons, he had rescued her from Elsa and a future as Lancel's mistress. In their short time together, she'd enjoyed this amazing, if dangerous, life of adventure.

But did all of it amount to true love? She couldn't honestly say.

"What, no answer?"

"He loves me more truly than any man ever has." The statement was definitely true and felt good to say, but it was not the answer she'd wanted to give.

"I have a question for you, thief," Waldo said. "Do you know of any Great Monster in or near here?"

"What, you mean other than goblins?"

"Right."

"There's the story about Willmon's Tower. Back in the duke's grandfather's day, he came up with the brilliant idea of building a whole line of fortresses in the marshes to keep an eye on the goblins. Willmon's Tower was supposed to be the first."

"What happened?"

"About what you'd expect. Halfway through building it, the thing fell into the marsh. The old duke tried to rebuild, but there was a fire, and it burned down. He tried a third time, and that one burned down and then fell into the marsh. The old duke finally gave up. Now they say the ruins are cursed, and some terrible monster lives there."

"Is this more than a rumor? Is there any actual proof?"

"You mean from people? No, there's no folk who live in the marshes. Goblins, though, are afraid of the place."

"I asked the duke if he knew about any Great Monsters, and he didn't mention this."

"Why would he? You think he wants a White Mage to go running off into the marshes on a werbil hunt? I'm sure you see killing monsters as a sport, but the last thing the duke would want is one of your kind dying on his doorstep." Cleptus had a sly grin. "Course, he might not be so reluctant now."

"I have no idea what you mean."

"What, you think I didn't notice you had his sword? Everyone in this city knows what it looks like. Kind of hard to miss with the gold thread and all. And you've already said you want to sneak out of Norwich. Hah, and people call me a great thief."

"The duke lent it to us of his own free will."

"Oh, yeah? Did he say you could keep it?"

In the flickering torchlight, they saw a coiled snake on the wall ahead.

"I have my reasons."

Cleptus nodded. "Don't we all?"

Passing in front of the snake, Cleptus deliberately stepped over a trip wire. Not noticing it, Waldo dragged his foot through the line, releasing it. There was a clunk. Cleptus broke into a run as the floor beneath them gave way. Waldo gasped as he fell. In the firelight, he got a clear look at the pit filled with sharpened spikes below.

"*Levitarus!*" Waldo spoke the spell barely in time. He levitated with his face no more than three or four inches from the tip of one of those spikes.

Meanwhile, Claptus was around the nearest intersection and gone from sight. His voice rang out clearly. "You should have made a deal with me wizard. Good luck to you finding a way out!"

Chapter 22

There Is No Easy Way Out

"We have a frog, a dog, a rat, and a duck," Alice said. Beneath the frog and dog were chalked X marks.

"I think it's a goose," Gronk said.

"No, it's a duck."

"Looks too big for a duck."

"All the drawings are about the same size, whether they're horses or snakes."

"I still say it looks more like a goose to me."

"I don't care whether it's a duck or a goose," Waldo snapped.

They had been wandering about the sewers for what felt like hours. Their torch went out, and Waldo was using a fire spell to let him see. Alice and Gronk both suggested he not bother as they could lead him through the dark. He'd decided to use some of his mana to maintain a small fire on the tip of his wand. He did not want to feel completely helpless. "We'll take the tunnel marked with the rat. We've already been through the ones with the dog and frog."

"You sure, darling? We haven't yet been down the one with the duck, either."

"Goose."

"We're going this way." Waldo took a piece of chalk and drew an X beneath the rat and then left the intersection to walk along the tunnel. Alice and Gronk were quickly right behind him.

"Make sure to keep an eye out for snakes on the wall," Alice said.

"I know," he muttered.

"I am just trying to help, darling."

"I know, I know." Waldo did not mean to take his frustration out on her.

He felt like a complete fool. He had let Cleptus outsmart him. It was the mob at the bridge all over again. Waldo assumed the thief could be no threat and got careless. As a result, he nearly died, again, and he and his familiars were lost in these wretched sewers. He could imagine his mother hanging her head in shame, a look of disappointment in her eye.

Wasn't he supposed to be better than this? The quest started off rather badly, but after escaping Middleton with Gronk, things improved. He still had to worry about his grandfather and possibly the White Mage, Melissa. Yet, he felt he got better at this whole adventuring thing. He had his brilliant disguise down and was spreading suspicion and doubt about the whites. Slowly he was discovering how to lead Alice and Gronk, despite not having proper Contracts with them. Waldo had also made the ingenious decision to rob the duke of his most prized possession before fleeing. Finally, he chose to use the thief not only to recover the money but to aid them in their escape. He even dealt with Cleptus's defiance in a way his mother would approve.

All those decisions were obviously the right ones. So how had things ended up this way?

Alice came to his side and placed a hand lightly on his arm. "It's all right, darling, you don't need to worry. Everything will work out."

"I'm not worried."

"Darling, there's no point to lying. I can tell what you're feeling." Alice wrapped her arms around his chest and hugged him. "I'm sorry."

Waldo was surprised and a bit uncomfortable. Those were not words he'd heard often from people who mattered to him.

"You don't have anything to be sorry about, Alice."

"Yes, I do. I let him take my purse. Then I made you come to the tavern to try and get it back. If it's anyone's fault we're here now, it's mine."

Waldo could sense her sorrow. He wasn't sure how to respond to it. His mother hadn't much cared about feelings. He slid an arm around the small of her back and pulled Alice a little closer. "I don't blame you for losing the purse. Gronk and I were both there, and we didn't prevent it. Going to the tavern wasn't a mistake. Cleptus stole from me. Trying to get the coins back was the right choice. Letting him get away was the only error. I am the master, and I am the one who makes the decisions. The responsibility for this is mine and mine alone."

Alice lifted an eyebrow. "You're not going to start saying I'm a familiar again are you?"

"No." *Though you are.*

"It's sweet of you to say, but still true that we ended up here because you listened to me."

"Do you mean I can ignore what you think from now on?"

"You missed my point."

"Will you at least Charm people whenever I tell you to from now on?"

"No. Look, darling, what I am saying is that I'm sorry I got so obsessive. But I know everything is going to work out fine. I trust you, and I know we will find a way out of here."

Hearing her did make him feel better, as did the way she was embracing him. Masters were not supposed to care what their servants thought. Yet, Alice's words made some of his worries melt away. It gave him the oddest sense he had done something right, despite the current situation.

"Alice, I made the choice. I could have said no. Even though you can be rather scary at times."

"Hey!"

"Oh, come now. We both know it's true. But despite your morals and silly notions, sometimes you are right."

"Only sometimes?"

"I still think you should Charm people whenever I say."

"It would be wrong."

"So you keep telling me. Still, I couldn't do without you. I am very glad to have you at my side."

He noticed her cheeks blush and a sense of happiness spilled over through the bond. She slowly rubbed herself against him. "Thank you, darling," she whispered in his ear. "When we get out of here, I promise to make it up to you."

"Does that mean you'll give me one Charm?"

"Ah, I had something else in mind."

"You mean that thing you do with your tongue I like so much?"

She gaped at him and looked back to where Gronk was. The ogre stood grinning.

"He means the way I kiss!"

"No, I don't."

"Yes, you do," she growled.

"Why are you angry all of a sudden?"

"I am not angry!"

"Yes, you are. In any case, I wasn't referring to kissing. I meant how you take your mouth and…"

Smack!

"Don't you dare say that where anyone else can hear! I'll die of embarrassment."

"Oh, please, sweetheart." Gronk chuckled. "Like anything should embarrass you. I mean, you did pleasure me with your feet once."

"WE NEVER SPEAK OF THAT AGAIN!!!"

XXX

In the meeting room, a single torch provided light. Daring sat with an empty mug in his hand across from his friend Markus. At other tables, several others sipped from their own mugs and looked on. Since his escape, Daring managed to empty about half a keg of brown ale. Daring still gazing at his left hand. "There's skin over the wound. It's not even red or scarred. How'd he do that? You'd think it was from years ago."

Markus answered him with one word. "Magic."

"Never knew a wizard could do such a thing."

"Yeah, they're amazing."

Daring kept staring at the nub where his pinky used to be. "Do you think if I cut his hands off he'd be able to heal them?"

"Who knows? It's not something I'd want to test."

"It's what I should do, you know... cut his hands off and leave him as a beggar in the streets."

"I'm sure he'd hate it." Markus took a sip from his mug. "You should have never gone anywhere near a White Mage. No matter how much gold he had, it wasn't worth it. 'You never try to shear the wolves.' You're the guildmaster. You're the one who taught us the basics."

"Don't remind me," Daring muttered. "I never would have if it weren't for her. You saw her. She was worth the risk."

"Still feel that way, Nine Fingers?"

"Funny man."

Markus paused and leaned forward in his chair. "You know we can't let this White Mage go. Sooner or later he's going to find his way out. Then what? We've all heard how ruthless they are. You think this one is simply going to forget about you? And if he returns for you, none of us will be safe."

"He won't be back. He took the duke's sword."

"You think it's any better if he sends one of his friends to do us in instead?"

"I get it. We'll end him. Him and his savage. My red haired beauty though… her I don't want hurt. Not a bruise, not a scratch."

"You want us to bring down a wizard and someone who can lift a wagon with one hand and be gentle with her while we're at it? You're asking a whole lot."

Daring sent his friend a furious look. "I am going to make her my woman, no matter what it takes. I want her more than any girl I've ever laid eyes on."

Markus raised his hands. "Fine, you're the boss."

"Damn right."

A few minutes later, one of his men came in to tell him they were coming.

"Bring the chest in here and get the lads ready. Make sure everyone knows not to be too rough with my lady."

XXX

"Do you hear something?" Alice asked.

"No," Waldo said.

"Yes," Gronk said.

Alice stopped and peered ahead. "Darling, could you extinguish your wand?"

"If I do so, I won't be able to see anything."

"Just for a bit."

With a frown, Waldo negated the spell. Once he did, they could all clearly see a flicker of light coming from twenty feet down the tunnel. The three of them made their way towards it as quietly as they could. The glow framed a doorway carved into the wall. Gronk reached out and gave a slight push. The door silently swung open.

"Not suspicious at all," Alice muttered.

"Come on," Waldo held his wand in hand and entered. "It's better than being lost."

They found themselves in an antechamber with another door. Waldo nodded to Gronk. This door, too, was unlocked. It opened wide to reveal a large room with four tables and multiple chairs. There was a single torch, its light not enough to reveal the entire room. At one of the tables sat Cleptus Daring with a large wooden chest.

Alice leaned close and whispered urgently in Waldo's ear. He listened and gave a nod.

"Did you enjoy wandering around the sewers, lord wizard? Are you willing to make a deal now? Come sit down, and we can talk."

Waldo spoke in a soft voice, only loud enough for his familiars to hear. Alice shut the door behind them, while Gronk took a couple steps to get between Waldo and Daring.

"You're not going to be rude and refuse, are you?" Daring popped open the lid to the chest. He grabbed a fistful of coins and let them slip away. Most had the reddish tint of copper, but a few shined of gold and silver. "Come sit. We'll work something out over a few mugs."

"Didn't I already tell you, thief?" Waldo said. "I won't bargain with you. *Ventus*."

A strong burst of wind blew out the sole torch and plunged the room into pitch blackness. Waldo, Daring, and the thieves who'd been hiding in the shadows were now completely blind. Gronk and Alice could still see perfectly.

XXX

Daring's plan had been simple: allow Waldo and the others to sit and relax, perhaps drink some ale. Then, when their guard was down, he would signal the boys, and the wizard and savage would die under a hail of thrown daggers, while Alice would not be touched. The instant things went dark, the plan got tossed aside.

He and his boys were used to the darkness. They were all experts at hiding in the shadows and moving about in silence. But human beings needed *some* light to be able to see. With all the hidden doors shut, the darkness was total. Not only could they not see, they were trapped in a room with a wizard. His lads were tough, but they were thieves not soldiers. They had only agreed to the original plan because as risky as it was, it seemed less dangerous than letting the wizard go. The idea of fighting a White Mage they couldn't see was more than a little bowel loosening.

The men all panicked.

"Someone light a torch!"

"No! Don't!"

"What do we do?"

"I say light it!"

"Kill 'em before they kill us!"

"Let's get out!"

"Can anybody see 'em?"

"Run! Run! We have to run!"

"What do we do? What do we do?"

"We got to kill 'em!"

"Where are they?"

"Gronk smash!" There was the unmistakable sound of wood being turned into kindling.

Beneath all the shouts, Daring heard a sound like something tearing.

"I want Cleptus alive!" the wizard cried. "You can kill the others."

"Got it, Master."

Daring was on his feet with a dagger in each hand. He wished he'd drunk less. "Calm down! There are only three of them, and we can kill a mage like any other man. They're as blind as we are."

"Really?" Alice's voice called out. "Then how do we know there are exactly twenty of you?"

Those words made his blood run cold. The wizard's magic let him see in the dark. Daring had badly underestimated Waldo. He was trying to decide what to tell the lads when he felt the floor shake. Then something like a brick smashed into the side of his face, and all his thoughts vanished.

XXX

Alice enjoyed seeing Gronk knock the damned thief out. If she had her way, she would do a lot worse. *Time for revenge later*. Alice was fully transformed, angry, and ready to do murder. She had no sympathy whatsoever for the men standing before her. When the three of them arrived they all skulked in the shadows with their weapons drawn, intentions obvious. Now they were helpless, she didn't feel any pity for them.

The first one she came upon held a short sword in one hand and a carving knife in the other. He faced the wrong direction and uttered something about needing to get out. He had no idea she was even there. One swipe of her left hand and her claws sliced open his throat as neatly as a kitchen knife would have a rabbit's. Blood pumped into the air. He dropped his weapons and clutched at his ruined neck.

It was her first time killing a man. Alice was surprised how little she felt. It was no different to her than killing that goblin. He'd been an enemy, and she'd dealt with him. It was as simple as that. She remembered telling her husband once how she would do absolutely anything to protect him. Those words had been true. The idea of these men wanting to kill Waldo infuriated her even more than the fact they'd wanted to kill her. Anyone who tried to hurt her husband was dead so far as she was concerned.

Alice didn't so much as spare her first victim a second glance. She ran to the next and stabbed him through the chest with the claws of her right hand. This one let out a scream as he died, and she got a face full of warm blood for her trouble. Number three she gutted like a fish.

On the other side of the room, Gronk was equally busy. He caved heads in with his fists, and she watched as he literally tore another man in half. The thieves who were still alive were screaming, trying to find out what was going on. Only a couple had stumbled about, frantically searching for what she assumed was a hidden door.

Waldo was sitting on the floor at the same spot where he'd cast his spell. Without light, he could not safely direct his magic, so he left the fighting to them. The strategy was fine with her, as she and Gronk could deal with this lot easily enough.

Number four got his head chopped clean off.

After scant minutes, it was over. Not one of them got away.

XXX

It turned out the meeting room contained five torches. Waldo lit them all and got a clear view of the carnage. The floors and walls were splattered with blood, and mangled bodies lay tossed about the room. The sight didn't particularly bother Waldo. He'd seen worse.

In one corner, Gronk had peeled the skin off the back of one of the corpses. He happily snacked on it and drained a keg of ale. Waldo approved. After such good service, his ogre had certainly earned a treat.

Alice, meanwhile, had dumped the contents of the treasure chest and was sorting through them. All the gold and silver coins got separated and counted. The pricess took longer than had the fight. "We got all our gold back," she said, smiling from ear to ear. "We also have seventy-five more silver coins, and I am guessing at least twenty thousand copper ones. For all our trouble, we wound up way ahead."

Waldo noted the gold and silver was put in a purse which Alice promptly tied back around her waist. The copper coins she began shoveling back into the chest.

Waldo stood over the unconscious form of Cleptus.

"What do you want to do with him, darling?"

"Take his shirt off and lash him to one of the posts." Waldo picked up a dagger from the floor. He noted the blade was quite sharp. "I have something very specific in mind for him."

Chapter 23

A Morio Seal

He was choking and gasping for air.

"Wake up, thief. The night grows short, and I have miles to go before I sleep."

Daring opened his eyes and spat out what was in his mouth. It took a moment to adjust to the light. When he finally did so, he found himself staring into a very young, very smug face with yellow eyes framed by hair of the same color. He lay on the floor, and his arms were tied to a beam. He swung his head around to either side.

Blood.

Blood everywhere.

He saw legs and arms and mangled corpses. There was Markus ripped in two. His guild, his friends, who'd been drinking and talking with him an hour ago were nothing but meat now. Sitting among the dead was a gigantic green-skinned beast with tusks. In one hand, it held a keg and in the other what looked like a hunk of skin. As he watched, the monster brought the still bleeding flesh to its lips and hungrily devoured it.

Daring turned away and fought the urge to vomit. "Is that an ogre?"

"Yes. His name is Gronk. I used my magic to make him appear as a female barbarian and as a male tough when we were in the tavern."

"He's eating one of my men!"

"Yes he is," the White Mage said with sickening calm. "He normally eats whatever he kills. Tonight he earned himself a feast."

It was too much. Daring turned his face to the side and threw up on the floor. When there was nothing left in his stomach, he turned back. His mouth tasted of puke, and his throat felt raw. "Damn you. How could you let an ogre do such a thing? You're a White Mage!"

"I did tell you my attitudes were a bit more liberal, didn't I?"

Daring then said something he hoped was the greatest possible insult to a white. "You're a complete monster."

"Thank you."

"Do you not like monsters? What a terrible surprise." Those words were from his beautiful lady. She had been standing behind the wizard, so he hadn't noticed her. Now she stepped into clear view.

His eyes widened, and he gagged. If there had been anything left in his belly, he would have brought it up. His beautiful lady was drenched in blood- her face, her hands, her arms, her clothes. She might as well been wearing red. But the blood was the least of it. She had *wings*! Like those of some sort of monstrous bat, they stretched and contracted with her every step. On each of her fingers sprouted a claw, and horns grew from the side of her head. The fangs he thought he'd imagined were back. He even noticed a tail lashing about behind her.

Yet the beautiful face was still there. Those exotic eyes and magnificent breasts and curves were all in place. When she moved, there was the same sensual roll to her hips. It was as if the gods were mocking him by leaving so much of her beauty in place, while attaching all of these hideous features.

She was disgusting.

Alice gave a knowing nod. "I can tell by the way you're looking at me exactly what you think."

"It can't be… you're a… a…"

She tilted her head ever so slightly. "Goddess?"

"Monster." The word came out in a sorrowful moan. This was what he had lost everything for? This horror? He'd been cheated. If he had known the truth, he would have never come near her.

"Does this change things for you?" She took three slow steps towards him. "Didn't you say you loved me? Surely your feelings haven't changed so quickly." She leaned down and reached a hand with those long claws towards him. "Don't you still want my touch?"

"No, please." He shut his eyes and turned away as much as the ropes would allow. Daring could feel the tip of one claw press against his cheek.

"Alice," the wizard spoke.

The pressure vanished.

"I was teasing him a bit, darling. I wasn't actually going to hurt him."

"I don't care if you hurt him. Don't kill or maim him too much until I've made my offer."

Daring opened his eyes and focused on the young wizard. As incredible as it might be, *he* was the least frightening one. No matter how bad the situation, Daring was still alive. As long as you were alive, there was hope. He would say and do whatever it took to get out of this. Daring grinned and did his best to actually sound composed. "Don't tell me after all this you're actually going to bargain with me?"

"No," the wizard told him. "I will give you a choice to make, but there won't be any bargaining. First, when we leave here, you're going to show us the way out. Don't think you have any say there, you don't need fingers or hands to give us directions."

Daring thought of the ogre munching on his friend and shuddered. "Right you are, lord wizard. I'll be right proud to lead you out of here."

"I am not a lord, and I don't care to be called a wizard. My proper title is Master Rabbit."

Daring bent his neck. "As you say, Mater Rabbit."

At this point the wizard brought out a dagger and slowly turned it in his hands. "After we are outside, the question will be what to do with you. The simplest option would be to kill you. Since you've tried to murder me, executing you would only be proper."

"I can already tell you I'm leaning strongly towards option two."

The White Mage continued to twirl the dagger. "You were able to rob Alice without her noticing. You were also able to escape her on the roof tops and all of us in the sewers. The fact you could get so many men to fight for you when you have no rank or authority is also impressive. You are a man of some skill, and a good thief could be very useful to me on my journeys. I would be willing to take you as my servant."

Daring let out a relieved breath. His luck still held. He was actually going to live through this. He would play along and do whatever he was told. Then, when the moment was right, he would disappear. If things played out a certain way, maybe he would even get the chance to cut the wizard's throat before he left. Daring bent his neck once more and tried to sound as sincere as possible. "I would be most happy to be your faithful servant."

"Delightful." The wizard tapped the side of the blade against his palm. "Of course, that leaves the question of how I can ensure you *are* a faithful servant. You're human, which means I can't form a Contract with you and make you a familiar."

"Thank goodness," Alice muttered.

"I could create a Death Seal, but it would seem a waste as I can only use the seal once."

"I am not sure what a death seal is, but I want to avoid anything with, 'death' in it. I will swear an oath in Wotal's name to you. No man would dare break such an oath." *Well at least no one who actually cared about pissing off the gods.*

"Oh, please. As if I would trust any promise coming out of your mouth."

"Wotal is a vengeful one. You don't swear oaths in his name lightly."

"I have more faith in my magic than I do in any foreign god." The wizard then sat in front of him and placed the blade against his chest. "Now, hold still. This won't take long."

"What are you doing?" Daring asked nervously.

"I am going to carve a morio seal into your chest, above your heart."

"What?!" Daring didn't dare move with a dagger hovering over him.

"It's a very special seal. It places a curse on your heart. Unless I chant a warding every three days, your heart will tear itself into pieces. So should you betray me or run away, I simply won't speak the chant and wherever you are, you will fall dead within three days. Obviously, the same will occur if you should kill me. I think this will do to ensure your loyalty."

Daring stared at him in horror.

"Feel free to scream as much as you like, but try not to move, or we will be here all night."

XXX

Gronk pushed the iron door open. It gave with a loud squeal from rusted hinges. The other side of the door was covered in moss and wild grass. When they stepped outside, it was still night time.

"I have never been so happy to see stars," Waldo said.

"We all smell like sewer," Alice complained. "And these bloodstains are never coming all the way out."

"I will buy you new clothes at the next city we visit. I can certainly afford it now." Not only had they taken the coins, they had also gathered all the weapons before setting out. It was a staggering number of short swords, daggers, and throwing knives. From where they were, Waldo could easily make out the walls of Norwich perhaps a mile behind them. "You did a fine job, thief. Now take us to Willmon's Tower."

Cleptus gave a sour grunt and rubbed his chest. He was not bound and was even armed. "It isn't so easy. I know the sewers like the back of my hand. I've never been in the marshes. I only have a vague idea where the ruins are."

"Which is still more than the rest of us have. Lead the way. I want to be as far from the city as possible when the horrible ball of fire rises."

"Of course, Master Rabbit." Still rubbing his chest Cleptus walked ahead.

Gronk, who remained in his true form, followed. Alice, who appeared human once more, hung back with Waldo. "You know, darling, you look really happy right now."

"Do I?"

Alice nodded. "You look like the cat that caught the rat."

Waldo stared at Cleptus as the thief trudged northward. "Alice, would you like to know a secret?"

"Sure."

He leaned to her. "There's no such thing as a morio seal."

Alice burst out laughing. Waldo laughed as well.

Chapter 24

A Bad Day

When Duke Griffinheart woke the next morning, it was the beginning of a glorious day. It took less than an hour for that to change.

"What do you mean they are gone?"

The sergeant struggled to meet his lord's eye. "They departed last night and have not returned, my lord."

"I left orders not to allow them to leave. Were my instructions unclear?"

"No, my lord," the sergeant said in a small voice.

"Did they overpower you somehow? Did the mage use some spell?"

"No, my lord, nothing like those things."

"Then why did you let them leave?"

The sergeant's eyes flickered all about the room. His mouth opened and closed soundlessly.

"Well?"

"The red haired woman. She… she talked to us and asked us to make an exception. She promised they would return before the dawn."

"And you believed her?"

"I know it sounds foolish, my lord, but I couldn't refuse her. It was as though she had bewitched me."

The duke's immediate instinct was to yell at the man and let him know what an absolute ass he was. And were it any other woman, he would have. But when Alice had visited him last night and asked for his sword he had handed it over to her. When the sergeant mentioned being bewitched Theos knew exactly what the man meant. "Were any of them carrying Lawgiver?"

When the sergeant nodded, Griffinheart felt sick. "The savage had it."

The duke was quiet for a long time. When he gave a half nod, the sergeant took it as a sign of dismissal and quickly departed. Griffinheart hardly noticed. He sat at the table without bothering to so much as touch his morning meal. The plight of the countryside being ravaged by an army of undead suddenly seemed insignificant next to his *real* problem.

Lawgiver was much more to him than a magical sword. It was a tangible symbol of his family's honor and status. The envy of other lords throughout Lothas. It represented the strength and greatness of his house. If he appeared in public without it, all would notice the absence. What was he to say? Tell them he had knowingly lent it to a woman, and she had walked out his front gate? He would die of shame. Theos would sooner claim to have misplaced it.

I will be a laughing stock to my own people.

He wanted to smash everything in sight. Silently he cursed the deceitful strumpet and wished he'd never heard of her. He damned that cowardly wizard and all of his kind, as well. Not only had Rabbit brought this plague down on his lands, he had fled rather than face the danger. Worse, he had stolen Lawgiver, deliberately humiliating him and his entire house. Theos couldn't begin to guess the reason. He had been more supportive of the whites than the majority of his fellow nobles. What could their purpose be in shaming him like this?

Many claimed the White Mages were deceptive and always scheming. It was said their order was consumed with secrets and conspiracies. He had never fully believed the tales. Now though, he could see all those stories were true. This theft could only be some twisted part of a much deeper game. He would notify King Leo. His grace needed to know what the whites were up to.

He was still seated at the table, consumed with thoughts of conspiracies and secret plots, when Sir Berrs arrived. The knight's suit of plate armor, clanked with each step. Theos didn't notice until he called to him a few times. "What was that?"

"I asked if I should have the servants bring you your armor, my lord. The men have assembled, and the crowds are gathering to see you lead them."

"Damn it, I'd actually forgot."

Sir Berrs's mouth gaped open. "You'd forgotten you were leading your forces into battle?"

"I can't now. Rabbit and his companions have disappeared. He used his magic to steal Lawgiver. I can't lead my men into battle without my family's blade in my hand."

The lie was not much, but it was a small salve to his pride. Having a wizard use his magic was more acceptable than admitting he'd given the sword to a woman with his own hand.

"He wouldn't dare," Sir Berrs said, clearly in disbelief. "He must know we would never forgive him or any of his order!"

"It's the absolute truth." Duke Griffinheart put two fingers over his right eye. "May Wotal strike me blind."

"What is to be done, my lord?"

"I want the city searched for any sign of Master Rabbit and his women. If they are found, they are to be returned here, unharmed is possible. Getting my sword back is what matters most. I'll not have my family name mocked."

"What about the troops? They are assembled and ready to march."

Theos shook his head. "Impossible. How can I lead them without Lawgiver? Every man will see it as a bad omen. They will say I am cursed."

"But, my lord, we have to march. Every hour we do not, the enemy grows larger. If we do not meet them on the field, they will eventually come here."

"Let them. They can smash themselves against our walls. No goblin force has ever taken this city. These abominations will fare no better."

"What of the villages surely to be overrun in the meantime?"

"We can do nothing for them."

With armor clinking, Sir Berrs fell to one knee. "Then my lord, allow me the honor. I will take the men out and rid the land of this pestilence."

Theos eyed Berrs suspiciously. His father was the Earl of Warwick, and he would assume the title in time. Berrs was an excellent knight with a good head on his shoulders. No doubt he could lead the soldiers well and defeat this dark enemy.

And claim all he glory for himself. What would the songs say? Noble Sir Berrs fought the horde of unnatural things while Duke Theos Griffinheart cowered in his keep. "Get up," Theos snapped. "No one will lead the men but me. I will not give you such fame."

Berrs stood. "I am thinking of the people, not about the honor."

"How very noble of you. Go and organize the search. If you can recover my blade, we will march. In the meantime tell the men to break ranks. They can help search or train."

"Yes, my lord."

XXX

Melissa had returned to the small village of Peabody and *finally* picked up the scent again. "A White Mage travelling with a woman named Alice and an ogre. You're certain?"

"It would be hard to forget," Lorimer said. "They came by before the solstice and rescued our missing children." The man gave her a rough bow. "We are truly grateful."

"I am glad he was there to help."

Melissa was in an awkward position. She could not, under any circumstances, admit publicly that Waldo was an imposter. If the story got out someone was pretending to be a member of her order, then people would start to question if the White Mages they met truly were White Mages. It might also give other magic users dangerous notions. Minister Barrows had given her specific instructions not to reveal the fact Waldo was an imposter to anyone outside of the Order. In his judgment, any harm Waldo caused could simply be denied and explained away as rumor. There were so many false tales about them already a few more wouldn't matter. Compared to the problems a rash of imposters might cause, it was better to pretend he was one of their own. After all, how much trouble could one man possibly make?

Sooner or later she would track him down and end his mischief.

Melissa was relieved to hear he had done some good. Saving those poor children and returning them safely was exactly what a true White Mage would do. But to go about with an ogre in his service? She could not begin to understand how he could he tolerate having such a thing near.

"He didn't accept any sort of reward?"

"He made a couple of jokes about taking one, but he didn't and set out right away."

"Towards Norwich?"

"That's right, Mistress Cornwall."

Curiouser and curiouser. He had robbed her and Master Roger but refused to take anything from these villagers. Did he only steal from fellow mages? *You are a strange one, Waldo Rabbit.*

"I beg pardon."

Melissa saw a little girl of eight or so cautiously approach. "Yes, child?"

"This is Jenna," Lorimer said. "She is one of the children Waldo rescued."

Melissa smiled down at the innocent child. "How lovely. What can I do for you, Jenna?"

"Is it true the White Mages are plotting to take over the world?"

Lorimer gawked at her, then at Melissa, and back again. "Jenna, you can't ask Mistress Cornwall something so rude."

"It's all right. I am not going to take offense." Melissa gently patted the top of the girl's head. "Tell me, dear, who told you that?"

"Master Rabbit! He told us not to trust any White Mages except for him."

"Why am I not surprised?"

"Do you know him?"

"Yes, as a matter of fact we first met only a matter of days ago."

"So the two of you are friends?"

"Friends? No, no, I am much more." Melissa caressed her wand as she spoke. "I am his fate."

XXX

Celton Poisondagger returned to his quarters following another dinner where he was seated among children. Every meal served as a public reminder of his low standing within the family. Relatives cast smug looks in his direction and refused to acknowledge his existence. From talking to father, he knew nothing would change. The knowledge did not make it any easier.

Outside the door to his rooms, his younger brother waited. "Murat," he greeted.

"Brother."

"Do you want something?"

"A few minutes of your time."

"All right."

They went inside. As soon as the door was shut Murat got right to his point. "Brother, when the time comes, I want you and your sons to support me."

"The time for what?" Celton asked cautiously.

"Our father is hale and hearty, and you know I wish he could live forever."

"Don't we all?"

Murat spoke slowly, measuring each word. "Yet we all know father will pass on at some point. When the sad day comes, who knows what will happen? Wouldn't it be better, wouldn't it be *safer,* if we were all united?"

Celton relaxed a bit. This wasn't a conspiracy. Murat was trying to find allies, and it only made sense he would turn to Celton and his sons. The other family members were dangerous. It was logical to try and protect yourself.

"We share the same mother, and I agree we should be united. But don't you think you should be supporting me? I am the older brother, after all."

"Age doesn't matter. Only strength counts."

"I am also more skilled."

"I am sure your proficiency comes as a great comfort as you listen to the little ones talk with full mouths."

"Is my place at the table what this is about, Murat? You think I've fallen and it means I will follow you now?"

"Brother, you *have* fallen." Murat held a hand up. "I am not saying it is just, but Father doesn't need to be just. You've been tainted with failure. You are no longer a candidate. I am not the only one who believes it is so. The entire family thinks the same."

"All of our positions change. We never sit at the same seat two meals in a row."

"But none of the other contenders have ever been exiled to the end of the table. You are literally as far down as you can be. No one will follow you now."

"Things can change."

"Not enough."

"You might be surprised."

"I have your answer, then? You won't side with me?"

"I agree we should make common cause, but you should support me."

"The rest of the family won't accept you as head. Not now."

"I think they will… and soon."

"Being stubborn doesn't change the reality of the situation, brother."

"Murat, you and the family don't know as much as you may think. My rise will be every bit as quick and spectacular as my fall."

His brother shook his head. "Father never forgives so easily. For now at least, let us agree to be allies. We can sort out who is following whom later."

"I can agree to those terms, I suppose."

As his younger brother departed, Celton had no doubt when the time for action came, he would be the one in control.

XXX

Walter lay naked on a table. On the chest, where the heart had been, the sewn up wound and seal were plain to see. Walter's body consisted only of the head, neck, chest, and abdomen. Charred remnants of bone and flesh were all that remained of the limbs.

Next to the table was a cart with a pair of arms and legs neatly severed and washed. Also on the cart was a saw, a pair of very sharp knives, an assortment of smaller hooks and scrapers, a large needle, and spools of thread.

Lilith hovered over her son, carefully examining the damage. She needed to reattach the arms and legs as cleanly as possible, or Walter would have difficulty using them.

"It doesn't look too bad. Once I have the new ones stitched on, I will reanimate them, and you should be fine. I expect you won't even notice the difference after a few days."

Walter's dead eyes stared up at the ceiling. It refused to acknowledge her.

"You know it's fortunate zombies can't feel pain. If you were alive, I expect your screams would have been heard from one end of the castle to the other. Assuming you survived."

Walter said nothing.

"As it is, in a couple hours I should be done, and you will be able to walk out of here in perfect condition."

She paused, but her son remained silent.

"You know, Walter, you could at least be a little appreciative of what I am doing for you."

Her prompts finally got a reaction as Walter's head jolted in her direction. "Are you joking? What should I be grateful for? You let Hera do this to me!"

"No," she said patiently. "*You* let her do this to you. I taught you better. From the moment you were allowed to put on the black robes, you were expected to protect yourself. Nothing changed simply because you died."

"How am I supposed to protect myself when I'm a zombie, and she is a necromancer?"

"Perhaps you should have considered the implications before confronting and threatening her."

"What would you do if she actually killed me?"

"You can't be killed. You are already dead."

"You know what I mean! What if she hadn't been satisfied with my arms and legs? What if she had burned me up completely?"

Lilith shrugged. "I'd have had the servants sweep you up and scrub clean the hall."

Walter stared at her. "Is that all?"

"What would you have me do? A soul can be summoned back to earth only once. It's why it is so important the container be protected." With one finger she thumped the seal mark written in her own blood. "If the container is destroyed or the seal broken, the soul is lost for good."

"Would you at least have avenged me and killed Hera?"

"Why would I?"

His teeth snapped at her.

"Stop acting like a child. Children can cry about how unfair the world is. Adults are expected to know better. You are going to have to deal with things as they are, not as you wish them to be."

"I thought she was going to destroy me. I really did. When she stopped, she said it was only because she didn't want to upset you."

Lilith inspected one of the hooks. "You might want to keep her words in mind from here on out. Hera is not going anywhere. If you want to survive, you are going to have to stop antagonizing her."

"You're saying I have to treat her as if I were a servant?"

"What I am telling you is you have to know your place."

"You can't trust her."

Lilith gave an annoyed sigh. "I don't trust anyone."

"But you're sharing your secrets with her," Walter whined.

"I am teaching her. I will show her only what I wish to. Believe me, I keep secrets from her as I do with everyone else."

"You care more about her than you do me."

She ran the hook against some blackened skin. It flaked off. Lilith gave a satisfied nod and returned it to the cart. "Now you really do sound like a child… and a spoiled one at that."

"You don't care about me at all."

"If I didn't, I wouldn't be going through the trouble of fixing you."

Walter glanced at the severed limbs on the cart. "I don't want them.They're the wrong size."

"They are fine. I took them from a healthy young slave named Tomas or Tamos. They will fit you perfectly." She picked the saw up and studied his left shoulder. "Now relax and let mother take care of you."

Lilith began sawing off what was left of his arm.

Chapter 25

Better Run Through The Marshes

They waded through hip-deep water. Except for Gronk. It only rose to his thighs.

Waldo shaded his eyes as he looked off to his right. "The group over there is now heading in the opposite direction. I don't think we'll need to worry about them." He pointed northwest. "There are still five of them about half a mile from us, but they've stopped." He pointed due west. "Probably more than a hundred of them are about two miles that way. It must be some sort of village. None of them are headed this way."

Cleptus glanced back towards Waldo and rubbed his chin. "Does he really know where all the goblins are?"

"We haven't run into any have we?" Alice said. "My husband's magic is amazing."

"Can't deny success, I suppose." Cleptus rubbed his chest absentmindedly.

Cleptus led them through the marsh, while Waldo and Gronk trailed behind. Alice's husband struggled to keep up the pace, and Gronk lent a hand now and again. Alice had decided to keep close to the thief. She didn't doubt he believed Waldo's bluff, but still wanted to watch him.

Having to trudge through warm water, mud, and grass taller than she was slowed them to a crawl. Stopping or changing direction to avoid goblins hadn't helped. If not for the trees, they could have looked back and still seen the walls of Norwich on the horizon.

"This is a huge mistake." Cleptus muttered. "Everyone knows better than to come here except when the army is around."

"You should have more faith in my husband." Cleptus glanced at her, and his eyes slid across her face and body. He silently chewed the corner of his lip.

"What?"

"Just wondering the sort of man he really is. My experience is what a man says is often a lie, but what he does will tell you the truth."

"I'll admit to having learned the same lesson. Who'd have ever thought we'd have something in common?"

"I think we might have a whole lot in common."

"I doubt it."

"Don't be so sure. I can be very charming when I want."

"Do you really think you're the first sweet-talking man I've ever met? I've known men whose mouths dripped honey."

"Is that how Waldo got you? With sweet words and promises?"

"You think he *seduced* me?" She couldn't help it. She burst out laughing.

"What's so funny?" Waldo asked from the back.

"Nothing. Cleptus thinks you're very seductive."

"Thank you, but I have no interest in men."

"It's true," Gronk said with a sorrowful lisp. "Master doesn't have a taste for snails. Least not yet."

"It's not what I meant at all," Cleptus said.

"There is no need to be ashamed," Waldo told him. "I take it as a compliment."

Cleptus sent Alice an exasperated look. She didn't feel any need to explain things. Having seen Waldo carve symbols into his chest and having gotten all their coins back, she no longer felt the need to inflict pain on the thief. Alice was willing to tolerate him, as he was now a part of their group. It did not mean she liked or trusted him.

"If he didn't win you over the old fashioned way, how'd he do it? Did he use a spell?"

"Certainly not. He never needed magic to make me his."

"So what did he do?"

"I used to be a barmaid at an inn. I was also an indentured servant. The very day we met, he made a declaration I would be his, paid my owner a hundred gold coins, and married me right then and there."

Merely recalling their first meeting made her heart thump. It had been the most romantic moment in her life, like having every secret dream suddenly made real. Of course it had turned out to be something other than what it first seemed, but nothing could change how she'd felt when Waldo spoke those words to her.

Cleptus's eyes widened. "He asked you to marry him the first time you met? And he actually paid a hundred gold coins for you?"

"He did."

Cleptus was silent for a few minutes as he kept slogging through the water. "I suppose," he finally said, "I can believe it. They say White Mages are rich, and I don't doubt some men would marry you on sight."

"Not you, though."

"There were lots of things I'd have done to you if I could, but I'm not the sort to marry."

"No, you're the sort to make all sorts of empty promises and tell a girl anything she might want to hear."

"Most women would call it being romantic."

"I have another name for it."

Cleptus clucked his tongue and gave a shake of his head. "So when did he find out?"

"What do you mean?"

"When did he find out what you really are? I don't pretend to be an expert about White Mages, but it's no secret what they do to monsters. Did he decide to make an exception because you were his wife?"

"You have it all wrong. He knew from the very start what I was. In fact he'd come to find me because I was a succubus."

"Then, why didn't he kill you?"

"Uhm…"

The reason was going to be a little hard to explain. Despite having forced Cleptus to join them, Waldo had decided not to tell him the truth about his identity or his goals. Cleptus was to continue believing Waldo really was a White Mage in service to Avalon. Her husband didn't trust the thief and didn't want him to know more than was absolutely necessary. "My husband is a very forward thinking person. He believes all monsters don't have to be killed on sight. Waldo feels we can help him in his battles. It is why he has me and Gronk and why we are searching for another to join us. After all, don't they say you should send a dog to kill a dog?"

"I suppose what you say makes sense, but why are you so pleased about it? He's only using you after all."

"No, he's not!"

"You admitted as much from your own lips."

"He isn't manipulative at all. He truly cares about me."

"You sure? Maybe the only reason he married you was to make you feel more loyal to him. I mean, it must be strange, to travel with someone who believes in killing your kind."

"You have it all wrong! He didn't even realize he was asking me to marry him."

"What? How could he not?"

"He's a foreigner. The very first words out of his mouth when we met were, 'I have come here to make you mine.' He didn't have any flowers with him when he said it. He meant it literally. I… I thought he was proposing, and when he paid to free me, I was sure of it. He said he'd come all the way to Stratford for me because I was very important to him." She twisted from side to side. Recalling his words made her want to melt. "He told me he was going to bind me to him, which I took to mean he was going to make me his wife. I had him perform the ritual our way, since I thought he was about to marry me using his customs. It turns out he used a spell to make me his familiar. But even though it was a bit confused, he did marry me, and I am his wife."

"So you're saying he never actually intended to marry you? All he wanted was to make you his servant?"

"Perhaps originally, but things have changed."

"How?"

"He treats me like his wife, not like a servant. He treasures me, respects me, and listens to what I have to say."

"Really?" Cleptus waved a hand. "So whose decision was it to come out here and search for some creature which may only be a story?"

"Waldo's, but there are plenty of other times when he listens to me."

"I'm sure about small things. I know all about making a woman happy. I'd let her have her way with whatever didn't matter to me, but I made all the important decisions."

"You don't know what you're talking about. Waldo always listens to me. He may not always agree, but my opinion matters to him."

"Or you simply think it does." Cleptus gave a sour laugh. "A slave in love with her master, how classic."

"I am not a slave!"

"Then why did he make you a familiar?"

Alice thought about the argument they'd had immediately afterwards. Waldo had insisted she call him Master and obey his every word. According to him, the binding spell *should* have made her obedient. Like a slave. It wasn't as if Waldo made any secret of the fact he didn't like having to actually compromise with her. Did he treat her like a wife because he truly loved her, or only because he was forced to?

The extended silence caused Cleptus to grin. "No answer?"

"Shut up."

XXX

A few hours later, the foursome stood on a muddy stretch of land. Waldo stared at a blaze of light on the horizon. At the pace they were going, it would take quite a while to reach it, but there could be no doubt. His third familiar was waiting for him.

XXX

Lucius Corpselover was bored.

All the villages near the city were now emptied. A small army of undead followed him. "I suppose it's time to visit Norwich."

Chapter 26

Come Tumbling Down

The riders came in shortly after dawn. They went directly to the duke's keep with the news. Not long after, all the bells in the city began to toll. The gates were shut, and men could be seen rushing all along the walls. In the streets, women and children ran about in confusion as husbands and fathers spoke tearful goodbyes.

Duke Griffinheart had his servants belt on the different pieces of his plate armor. The chest was a tight fit, but so long as he could breathe, it would do. One of his retainers brought him a scabbard. Theos made a show of pulling the blade out a few inches and inspecting it.

"Good steel." He slapped the sword back into its plain sheath.

The man tied it on without comment. All his servants were working with a bare minimum of speech. Griffinheart knew what they were thinking.

XXX

He stood upon the battlements above the gate, where all of his people could all see him.

The pikes with the goblin heads had already been taken down and handed out to the troops who remained unarmed. The duke had roughly thirteen hundred men under his command. Of those, only twelve were knights and four hundred were full time soldiers. All the rest were militia, men expected to arm and train themselves. Most of them wore no armor and carried staves, axes, long knives, clubs, and a wild assortment of other weapons. The men who had arrived from the countryside had been empty handed and got handed pikes.

Theos stared down at them. They had been assembled behind the gate with some of the knights there to command them. If things went well, he would throw open the gate, and they would go out to deliver the death blow. Theos would only venture forth once the battle was decided and the enemy completely disorganized. Every man born in Lothas was taught how to fight and knew he might be called upon to serve against the goblins. The majority were old enough to have marched the last time the army was raised. He did not doubt their courage or willingness to fight, only their discipline.

One well-trained, well-armed soldier was worth at least five militia in the field. Theos would rely on his regular troops to fight this battle. All along the ramparts were cauldrons filled with pitch, piles of brick and stone, and quivers stuffed with arrows. His soldiers had all been trained to use longbows. The walls of Norwich had never been breached. Its gate had never been broken. Ten thousand goblins could not take this city. The undead horde would smash itself against his walls. Archers would pick some off. Others would burn with pitch or be smashed with falling stones. And when only a few remained, he would open the gates and lead the brave men at his back to glory.

Theos spread his hands on the stone battlements. He would win this battle and save the city. The duke knew the story about his lost sword had gotten out, and now all could see he was without Lawgiver. He could feel the eyes of his men digging into his back. Theos could guess what they were thinking. Their liege lord allowed the symbol of his power to be stolen on the eve of battle. Could there be a worse omen?

It doesn't matter. I'll win this battle despite what the coward and his whore did.

XXX

The quiet unnerved Theos more than anything else.

In his life he'd had plenty of experience against goblins and bandits. As a young knight, he'd even visited Torikai and once fought in the Grand Tournament. Whenever goblins gathered for a serious battle, they took up a chant to drive themselves into a frenzy. "Grum, grum, grum," they chanted, sometimes for hours. Then from their throats would come deafening screams to make any man shake. The beasts then charged mindlessly into battle. Men always talked as they fought. They boasted, shouted, cursed, threatened, begged, cried, screamed in pain or in fury. Fighting for your life brought everything out. Even fighting in a tournament, you were surrounded by sound.

Now in the fields before his city an army approached, and it was silent. The only thing you could hear were their steps as they stamped down the grass on either side of the road. As he watched, they spilled from the woods. The first was the lich he'd heard about. It wore black robes with a pair of glowing orbs within its hood. Following behind it were the other undead. They followed after like sheep after a shepherd. At first you could see individual bodies, then small groups, and before long there was just a mass of them shambling out of the wood.

Most of them had to be long dead for they were mere skeletons. Perhaps one in five was a walking corpse. They carried no weapons. There was no order to them, no line of battle. They were no more than a mindless throng following behind the lich. It was a hot summer day and each small breeze filled the air with rot. Every breath was nothing but the overpowering stink of corruption. Theos was familiar with it. It was the aftermath of battle, when bodies had been left to rot for days after the slaughter. Either because you didn't have enough hands to bury them, or you didn't care to. Even to a veteran like him, this sickening pall was almost too much. He barely kept from bending over and tossing up everything he had in his belly. Across the battlements he saw many of his men doing just that. Even many of the men lined up behind the gate vomited.

Theos deliberately ignored it. He couldn't blame them, and calling attention to it would only shame them needlessly. If the smells weren't bad enough, the sight might unnerve a man. He'd heard the stories about undead since he was a child. Growing up so close to Alteroth, he knew the tales about the black wizards and their disgusting practices. He'd never actually seen one until now, though. Watching the dead shuffle along below him was truly sickening. These had been people! His people! They had either been murdered or brought back from their rest. This was an abomination in the eyes of gods and man. If Waldo and the other whites were truly behind this, then they were every bit as foul as the darks.

What Theos knew about the undead came from the stories. They were slow moving but never tire nor needed rest. They existed to kill all living folk and knew no pain nor fear. The only way to stop them was to smash in their skulls or incinerate them. The dead kept coming until they were destroyed or until they'd killed every living person in sight. The stories all agreed the dead could not climb walls or cross running water.

When they stopped coming out of the woods, Theos estimated their number at five or six thousand, a good sized army. The lich came to a halt well outside of bow range. The other undead stopped when they neared it. None would go a step further. The undead kept shuffling ahead until they were tightly packed, one great mass of corpses standing behind their master.

Theos could see his men pointing and talking to one another. Many drew circles over their hearts to ward off this evil. They huddled together and stared into the field. He heard their murmurs. The tone if not the words were clear to him. "Steady men! There's nothing to fear!" He called out in a loud, clear voice. "We'll wipe out these foul things, never doubt it. Stand to and be ready to fight."

His words appeared to have the desired effect. The archers got back into their lines. For a leader, half the job was making sure the men kept their heads. Keeping calm was a challenge in a regular battle. Facing these monstrosities, it was even more important.

The black robed creature advanced alone. Where all of the others shuffled and staggered, it walked like a man, with steady, certain purpose. The sight sent a chill straight through his guts. Theos was sure he was not the only one who felt this sense of dread. "Arrogant," the duke muttered under his breath. Liches were frightening creatures because they were a combination of undead and black wizard. They terrified because they could use all sorts of unnatural magics. His men had grown up with the same stories he had.

"If it wants to come stand beneath our walls we'll give it a proper welcome. Archers, light!"

Up and down the wall, sergeants repeated the command. By each squadron of archers was a lit torch. The men placed the tips of prepared arrows into the flame where they caught.

"Nock!"

The order was again repeated by a series of voices. The men placed their arrows against string.

"Draw!"

As one, they pulled back on the strings and lifted their bows into the air.

Theos watched the lich stride into range and continue forward at a steady pace.

"Hold!" He wanted the lich closer.

It continued to walk towards them.

"Hold!"

He guessed it was within two hundred and fifty yards. Then two hundred and forty, thirty, twenty, ten.

At two hundred, it advanced into easy range.

"Loose!" The duke cried out.

Loose! Loose! The call resounded up and down the rampart. Twangs reverberated as hundreds of draw strings were released. The air filled with flame arrows arcing into the sky, to rain all around the lich.

XXX

Lucius Corpselover heard the lord's orders as Lucius approached. Seeing all the flame arrows came as anything but a surprise. He stopped and watched as they fell. The nearest ones struck his barrier spell and bounced away. *Did those savages actually think their arrows could touch me?*

Arrows glanced away and the ones that struck further out set the grass on fire. With wand in hand he cast a simple spell. "*Velar est akua.*" A thick mist formed over the ground and quickly smothered the flames. "You barbarians have no concept of what magic can do."

Lucius continued walking until he was within thirty yards of the gate. Despite his poor vision, he was sure there were wide eyes and gaping mouths on many of the faces above him. No more arrows rained down. The liege lord seemed uncertain. Lucius was near enough to be easily heard. "I have no interest at all in your city."

"Then why have you come here?" the leader demanded. "Why have you done all this?"

"For Waldo of the white robes and his familiars. Send them out to me, and I will spare your city. All of you can live."

"So it's true, then? Waldo really is behind you and all your vile crimes?"

"Yes, he is the cause. I am here because of him. Now send him out."

"You're too late! Your master has already fled. My men have searched everywhere within Norwich and found no trace of him."

"You think Waldo is my master?" Lucius laughed. If he'd still had eyes, they would have watered. "What sort of lies has the boy been spreading?"

"He never admitted to anything. I pieced together the truth."

These people truly are idiots. "Whatever you believe makes no difference. Are Waldo and his familiars truly gone?"

"Yes, there has been no sign of them for two days. The coward ran away as soon as I told him we would ride out to face you."

"Then the lad has a good sense of survival." Lucius tapped his wand into his other hand. "Though his not being here is rather annoying." *Now what?* Lucius had hoped to draw his grandson out, but despite dressing like a White Mage, the boy wasn't stupid enough to behave like one. If Waldo left two days ago, then he needed to find the trail again as soon as possible. He had no further use for his undead minions. They were useless for tracking and would only slow him down. With Waldo gone, the city meant nothing, which was a shame since the walls were not warded and so completely vulnerable to magical attack. He gave a shrug of his bony shoulders. "Oh, why not? I am already here." Lucius held out his wand. "*Ossum paros lutum.*"

To the right of the gate, the base of the wall transformed from gray stone to ordinary dirt. There was an ominous cracking, followed by a hundred-yard stretch of wall come tumbling down. Mixed in were the amusing screams from the unlucky soldiers manning that section.

Lucius turned around and walked away. He sent out some mana to give orders to his servants. "Enter the city and kill every living thing."

As one, the undead stumbled forward to obey. They parted to allow him to pass as they continued to the breech in the wall. Behind him, Lucius heard the liege lord and others shouting orders to rally their troops. There was no chance they would keep his servants out entirely, but they might defeat them in the end. Undead actually didn't make very good combat troops, especially unsupervised. Depending on whether the defenders broke or not, the city might survive.

Lucius didn't care. Tracking down Waldo was his only concern.

Chapter 27

The Third Familiar

They found a road in the marsh. It was a simple dirt trail beginning in the middle of nowhere and running in the direction of their goal. Waldo assumed it had to be a remnant from the attempt to fortify this place. After all, what good was a fortress if you could not supply it? Now that they had solid footing, he was actually the one out in front leading the others. Alice was at his side with Gronk and the thief trailing after. He was so excited he could hardly wait. To his eyes a reddish light blazed ahead, perhaps only half a mile away now. It was every bit as bright as what had come from Alice or Gronk. There could be no doubt at all this was his third familiar. Once it belonged to him, a part of his quest would be completed, and he would be in excellent position to deal with the rest.

What would it do for his reputation back home when they learned he had three Great Monsters as familiars? It was very rare for even the heads of families to contract with more than one. Even his mother kept only Enver at her side. Without a doubt, people would start thinking he was amazing. Once they found out of course… which wouldn't happen until his return. Until then, they would continue to think of him as a fool, if they bothered to think of him at all.

A couple days ago, as they'd been stumbling about blindly in the sewer, he'd seen himself as a failure. Now though, everything was on track. He stared at the lovely reddish light ahead. His mind was swirled with ideas about what to do once he had all three Great Monster familiars with him. Who knew? Maybe he'd even get the contract right this time. With such powerful monsters serving him, defeating a knight would be no problem at all. The next big challenge would be tracking down a dragon's lair where he could try and steal an egg. That would be difficult enough, as dragons were resistant to most magics and impossible to scry on. Their lairs were always well hidden and near impossible to find.

And even getting close would be the *easy* part. Dragons were creatures of almost godlike power and ferocity. Whatever the stories said, a single hero or handful of heroes could not possibly fight a full grown dragon. Well, they could fight. There simply wasn't any chance they could win. To have any real hope required an entire army, with thousands of soldiers and at least a dozen mages. Even then, victory was not certain, and if you won, it would likely cost you half or more of your forces. If he vastly improved his magical skill, if his third familiar turned out to be a giant or a blood thirsty vampire (oh, Dark Powers, please!) Waldo understood facing a dragon was still impossible. He would need to sneak into the lair, steal the egg, and escape without confronting the mother.

Maybe I could acquire some slaves and use them as a distraction.

Waldo was not even thinking about the capture of his third monster. Already having two at his side, he was sure he would manage it somehow. His mind spun far beyond to the really hard part of his quest.

"Darling, I want to talk to you about something."

Waldo was wrenched back to the present. "Yes?" He noticed Alice had a handful of hair and was tugging at it.

"You... you know even though we argue sometimes and I get angry, I am still very happy to be your wife. There is no one else in the world I would rather be with. You are my ideal husband."

"Yes, I know." She immediately stopped tugging at her hair, and he felt annoyance through their bond. He didn't understand the reaction since he was agreeing with her.

"That's how you see me, too, isn't it darling? I mean, you see me as your beloved wife, not as your familiar. Right?"

Waldo nodded. "I do see you as a wife."

He saw her hesitate and take a deep breath. "I love you."

"Yes, I know."

She stopped walking. "Is tht reallyall yu have to say?"

Waldo was forced to stop as well. "Thank you?"

That was evidently the wrong answer, as Alice planted her hands on her hips and sent him a look he was all too familiar with.

"What was I supposed to say?"

"Nothing! It's not like I wanted to hear you tell me you love me, too."

"Fine. I love you, too."

Alice tapped her foot.

"What?"

"You don't mean it. You're only saying it because you think you have to."

"Obviously. Now can we get back to finding my third familiar?"

"Do you care more about finding this monster than you do about my feelings?"

"Yes."

She blinked, and he could feel surprise through the bond. "How can you say that?"

"Simple. You're always upset with me for one reason or another. So there's not much point in my worrying about your feelings. In any case I already have you, so obviously my priority is getting this last monster."

Her eyes narrowed, and for a moment, he was absolutely sure he was about to be kicked. Alice then continued down the road, her back and arms as rigid as pieces of iron.

"Master."

Waldo turned to see Gronk standing there. "What?"

The ogre stuck one finger at him and poked the air. "Badger!"

"Right."

XXX

The road ended before a stone archway. It might have been a gate once. Sections of wall still stood, and the base of what was perhaps an archers' tower. Other than those fragmanets, there were piles and piles of stone blocks covering most of the ground.

There were also bones… lots and lots of bones. From the littered skulls, Waldo could tell most of them were goblin, though there were a few human ones mixed in, as well. They were scattered everywhere, the remains of hundreds of creatures.

"Fuck me," Cleptus muttered. "Was there a battle here? Is that why it was abandoned? The stories don't say anything about a fight."

Waldo casually picked up a thigh bone and examined it. There were teeth marks. "This has nothing to do with battle." Waldo tossed the bone aside. "My new familiar is a messy eater."

"It ate all these things?"

"Yes. Isn't it marvelous?"

Cleptus gaped. "You're happy about this?"

"Naturally, why wouldn't I be? My final familiar is a predator with a taste for goblin and human flesh. What master wouldn't be happy about such good fortune?"

Shaking his head, Cleptus walked back the way they had come.

"Where do you think you're going?"

"Away from whatever did all this."

"If I die, you will only live one more day, you know."

"Still longer than I expect if I stay. If you survive, come collect me."

"You're a coward!" Alice snapped.

He stopped, turned around, and gave her a bow. "I prefer to think of it as being sane." He continued to walk away.

"Want me to drag him back, Master?"

"No, it's fine, I want him for his thieving skills not for his fighting. I depend on the two of you to capture this monster for me. Speaking of which, I want you to try and be as gentle as possible. This monster will be joining us after all, so try and do as little harm as you can."

Alice glanced about at the bones. "Right, gentle."

"You may as well transform now."

Alice did so, taking on her true form.

Gronk cracked his knuckles. "Don't worry, Master. I won't be too rough."

Waldo took out his wand. "Great Monsters who are in the wild are notoriously hard to capture. I expect it to resist fiercely. I can't think of anything more dangerous than a feral beast fighting with all its strength to remain free. Subduing it will definitely put both your lives at risk. Keep in mind, no matter how dangerous and brutal things may get, I want you both to be careful not to hurt my new familiar any more than necessary."

Alice rolled her eyes. "I am so glad to hear how worried you are about this other monster's safety."

"I've learned to be more thoughtful." He walked towards the archway.

Despite a look of annoyance, Alice followed on his heels, and so did Gronk.

Past the arch there were only more blocks of stone and gnawed bones. On this side, the stones were not only all over the ground but in several large piles. The biggest was the size of a small hill. Waldo pointed at one of the lesser piles. Without a word, both Gronk and Alice slid past him and got between their master and where the monster was still hidden.

Waldo cleared his throat, directing his voice towards his intended familiar. "Greetings. My name is Waldo Rabbit. I am a powerful mage and have come here to make you my familiar. If you will agree to serve me, I will promise you my protection and care. I already have an ogre and succubus. They can both assure you I am a fine master." He motioned to them.

"Master is the best," Gronk said. "He is cute and funny, provides seven or eight meals a day, and really knows how to handle a whip."

Alice shook her head, voicing her opinion grouchily. "Yeah, he's the best. He always appreciates you and would never put you in danger simply to get something he wants."

Waldo nodded.

"It's not like he would ever ignore your feelings or take you for granted or behave like you don't matter to him at all or..."

"Thank you Alice," Waldo interrupted, giving her the sort of annoyed look she normally offered him. Refocusing on the aura behind the stones, he spoke again, "You may as well come out now. With my magic, I know exactly where you are. If you don't, my familiars will have to drag you out by force. I would prefer you join me willingly, but I have come here to make you mine. There is nothing you can do to prevent it."

For some reason his last few words made Alice flinch.

There was no response for a moment. Waldo was about to tell Gronk and Alice to have a look, when they heard a grunt and the sound of movement. Scrambling from the other side was a wart covered creature with a long needle nose, bloodshot red eyes, a mouth filled with razor sharp teeth, and long, fetid black hair. It stood nearly as tall as Gronk with most of its length coming from its protracted limbs. It climbed to the top of the stone pile with ease and held a massive granite block over its head.

Waldo recognized it immediately, exclaiming joyously, "A troll! It's a-"

"Wah!" The troll heaved the stone directly at Waldo. The boulder rolled through the air, whistling like a bolt from a crossbow. Before he could even think, he was thrown to the ground. He had barely enough time to look into Alice's fearful eyes before the slab of rock caught her and spun her like a top.

XXX

Gronk knew what kind of strength was needed to heave so much solid rock, so it came as no surprise when he saw Alice's shoulder catch the brunt of it, and she hit the ground unmoving. Waldo stared in shock at his pretty little wife while he struggled to rise. He didn't have time for more than one look before the troll threw himself into the air, ready to rend and sever Gronk's master as he had so many others. Despite the size, the troll was quick and agile, the long limbs were muscled and possessed the smooth, predatory movements of a treecat. Landing cleanly, the troll took two quick steps. Gronk reached for the beast, grabbing at his greasy, matted hair. Turning with an unnatural flexibility, the troll slashed wildly across Gronk's chest. To Gronk's surprise there was pain... and blood.

The ogre slammed a fist right into the side of the troll's face and sent it tumbling back. A punch like that would have killed a man instantly and left his skull in pieces. The troll took it well enough. He stumbled but never lost his balance. Keen and furious dark red eyes never left Gronk.

The wart covered jaw hung loosely, wobbling disjointed and unhinged. The resprite gave Gronk a moment to collect his wits, his eyes going over to his master crawling to Alice and calling to her. "Alice…" He put a hand to her shoulder and quickly spoke the words to a spell. The fingers and palm glowing. "Oh, Alice, no…"

Gronk glanced down to his chest where five thin cuts seeped blood. The cuts weren't deep, but they stung badly. This was the first time that anyone or anything had ever been able to cut his skin.

"You're a nasty thing, huh, sweetheart?"

The troll prowled around Gronk, more cautious than before. One hand slapped at the loose jaw and shoved it back into place. There was a tearing sound of bone and flesh rending, like when Alice transformed. After just a moment, the troll snapped his jaw and howled.

"This isn't going to be easy is it?" Gronk whispered thickly, trying to absorb what he was seeing.

The troll's shoulders hunched, hooked claws clicking together as it hissed at him. Sliding to the right, red orbs fixed intently on Gronk's wound. A long slimy tongue licked lips.

"Not big on conversation are you? Reminds me of why I left the clan."

Gripping the ground till its nails broke the earth, the troll pounced at him, hands outstretched.

Despite his lisps and carefree attitude, Gronk had survived many fights with his life on the line. He stood, holding his ground, fists cocked. The sword strapped to his thigh was annoying, he even considered tossing it to allow his movement to be freer. Human weapons didn't come close to the power of an ogre's fists, so why even have it? The troll lunged. Gronk stepped forward and got inside his opponent's reach and planted his right hand firmly on the troll's neck. "Time to quit if you don't want to die."

"No quit!" The troll spat. The monster lashed out while Gronk tightened his grip. The troll's hook-like claws cut into Gronk's face and arm.

"Suit yourself." Gronk gave one hard, quick jerk of his hand, followed by a loud snap. The head rolled to the side at much too sharp an angle. The neck was most definitely broken. Gronk threw it to the ground and stepped back. The legs and arms twitched, but those blood tinted orbs weren't losing any of their menace. It was like the damn thing didn't know it was dead.

Then one hand grabbed the top of his head and rolled it back into place. Again there was the sound of muscle and bone knitting.

Gronk got a sick feeling. "Master," Gronk called. "I think we have a problem."

Waldo was kneeling over Alice, hands glowing. All his attention was on her. "Alice... please, Alice answer me."

"Master!" Gronk roared, stomping his foot so hard it shook the foundation and tumbled loose rocks.

Waldo at last looked up, noticing his ogre was bleeding. "Gronk, are you all right?"

The troll climbed back to its feet, shoulders hunched and head shifting from side to side with ease.

"No, definitely not. This thing does not want to die."

"It's a troll, Gronk. They're famous for their ability to heal rapidly. They're known to be able to survive almost any injury. They can even regrow limbs in a few hours' time. The only sure ways to kill them are to take their heads off or burn them to ashes. Fire is their one great vulnerability."

"Really could have used that information a minute ago."

The troll crouched eyeing him, hands opening and closing.

"Fine. This time I'll just rip his ugly head clean off. That should do it. Right, Master?"

Waldo glanced at Alice who remained unconscious. "I still want him alive, Gronk."

"Master, in case you haven't noticed, this thing's not tamed!"

"I know he's dangerous. It's what makes him so valuable." Waldo hesitated. "Please, Gronk, I need him to be my third familiar. We can train him later, but this is the only chance I will ever get to have a third Great Monster."

All the cuts were burning, and Gronk could feel blood dripping down his face, arm, and chest. Despite his wounds, Gronk nodded while keeping a careful eye on his adversary. "If that's what you want, I'll do it for you Master, but can you tell me how? Even if I can hold him down long enough, you think you can kiss him without getting your face bitten off?"

"The sword." Waldo pointed at Gronk's hip. "It's magical, remember? A troll's hide isn't as hard as a tree trunk. The blade should cut right through him."

"But this thing heals so fast-"

"If he's missing all his limbs, he'll survive but be helpless for a good long while!" Waldo pressed urgently, "Cut off his legs and arms, then hold his mouth shut. I'm sure I'll get the Contract right this time. Once I have him under my control-"

"No be pet!" The troll cried and charged at Gronk. The ogre whipped the sword out of its scabbard with three fingers, unable to hold it with more due to its human length hilt. In his beefy hand, it looked more like a long thin dagger than a true sword. The troll skittered along the ground, spiderlike and twitching, keeping just out of Gronk's reach. Attention clearly drawn to the blade.

"I feel ridiculous!" Gronk complained, swinging the sword as one might a paring knife. "How can you humans even fight like this?"

"I don't know. Wielding a broadsword was never a part of my education."

The troll leapt.

Not knowing what to do with it, Gronk simply held the blade in front of himself. The monster could not change direction in midair and was skewered through its bony chest.

Like some crazed beast, it howled and spat and desperately beat against Gronk to get free. Gronk obliged by yanking the sword out. Blood spurted, washing over his hand and forearm and spilling down the troll's chest. Falling on his back, the troll's shrieks were so loud birds and other creatures fled from nearby.

Gronk slashed at it. What his strokes lacked in precision or technique was made up for in raw strength. Again and again, the ogre chopped down. The troll tried to scramble away, putting up one hand as a shield while reaching around with the other. The sword cut easily into the troll, but each wound began to close almost as swiftly as it was made. Finally, Gronk managed to get in one good clean swing to hack off the troll's arm immediately above the elbow.

Gronk felt nothing but joy at seeing the creature writhe in pain. "I think I'm starting to get the hang of this!" As Gronk lifted his sword arm again, he missed what the troll had been flailing for: A huge melon sized stone. Swinging in a perfect arc, it bashed against the side of Gronk's head. The stone crumbled to pieces but knocked the ogre over.

Another rock was grabbed and smashed against Gronk's head.

The troll didn't have the leverage, but it had the raw power and the frenzy of pain and rage on its side. In a slow, haphazard tumble, Gronk collapsed to the ground groaning.

XXX

Waldo saw Gronk fall. Thanks to their bond, he knew Gronk wasn't dead, only unconscious, but that was bad enough. Both his familiars were down and in serious danger. He had to do something. "*Ventus*." His wind spell struck the troll, but other than make its hair whip about, had no effect. The spell did bring Waldo back to the troll's attention. The monster tossed aside the rock in its hand and stood up to his full height. Waldo was about ten feet from it, between the troll and a still unconscious Alice. Both Gronk and Alice had been hurt trying to protect him. Now it fell upon him to protect them.

He'd made too many stupid assumptions. Waldo had won over both of his familiars despite not having fully functioning Contracts with them. He'd seen how strong they were and had been sure they'd be able to catch this third monster for him.

Maybe there was a reason capturing even one Great Monster was such an achievement. His mother was the most powerful necromancer in the world, and even she was satisfied with only Enver. How stupidly arrogant was he to believe he was entitled to not one or two, but three Great Monsters?

Gronk and Alice were truly loyal to him. How many times would he have died by now without them? They served him not because they were compelled to, but because they truly wanted to. They were both precious to him, and he didn't want to lose either. No third monster would be worth such a sacrifice.

"I have fire magic. *Pyro*." A candle-sized flame came to life on the tip of his wand.

The troll stood still, clinking the claws of its remaining hand together. Its eyes stared at the small fire.

"I can destroy you."

The troll bent into a crouch.

"Walk away and leave me and my servants in peace. I will not try any further to force you to join me, but I won't let you hurt them either. Since I am giving up trying to capture you, there is no reason to continue fighting."

The troll's head slowly bobbed from side to side.

"No need fight. Man with fire go, ogre go, girl stay. Hungry is, girl smell sweet."

Saliva dripped messily down its chin. Wide cheeks pushed back with tittering and mocking giggles, it took a single step forward.

"You can't have Alice. If you're hungry there's a human thief not too far from here. You're more than welcome to him. But my wife comes with me."

"Want girl, her blood, her meat." The troll took another step forward.

Waldo came to a very easy decision. "Such a waste. *Pyro!*" The candle flame turned into a stream of fire that struck the surprised troll and ignited him, turning his whole body into a blaze.

"Wwwwaaaggghlar!"

Waldo had never seen anything ignite so fast. It could not have burned more fiercely if it had been dipped in pitch. To his horror, though, the troll refused to lie down and simply die. It stumbled forward, screaming in its death throes.

XXX

Bones slid against each other under her shoulder. Impaling pain robbed her breath as she tried to gauge what happened to her and what made the annoying noise. There was heat, and a foul smell of burning compost.

She opened her eyes and saw fire, moving fire, howling with pain, but what took her breath away was not only the engulfed form trying to reach her, but Waldo pulling at its leg, bare handed and burning to keep it from clawing at her.

"Darling…" she whispered.

Worry and horror filtered through their bond. She could sense it as real and alive as any emotion she ever felt. Waldo was in excruciating pain, yet he refused to let go. His hands were burning, but he wouldn't let go.

All to keep this fiery pyre from reaching her.

In a final, desperate swipe, the troll threw his arm backwards to snatch Waldo by his throat. Alice knew it was too late, the troll's arm whipped around too fast even if she could move. Her husband's eyes closed, and fear came flooding through her bond with him.

But the hand never reached him. The arm dropped off and the living pyre stopped moving, stopped howling. It collapsed. Ashes fluttered into the air. Crumbling to nothingness, the troll's limb, torso, and head all simply disintegrated.

XXX

Soothing energy flooded her, dampening her sharp pain to a numbing ache. Trepidation filled her bond, laced with nervous uncertainty. The light from his hands hurt her eyes, yet she could not fault him for it. "Does it hurt?" he asked, his voice tinged with concern. His hands were still red and raw. He had only healed himself enough to get full use of his fingers. Staring at him as he continued to poke and test certain parts of her shoulder and arm, she felt completely at ease.

"I was able to set the bones but soft tissue damage is something I want to heal only after I see to Gronk. You shouldn't be in any more pain. I need to conserve my mana until we're out of this marsh. I am sure-"

Alice leaned over and kissed him.

He looked absolutely confused. "What was that for?"

"You destroyed your third familiar to save me."

"To be honest, it wasn't just you. It wasn't exactly cooperating, and it would have also done who knows what to Gronk and me. I didn't really have much of a choice. I-"

"Darling?"

"Yes?"

"Sinply say, 'Yes, I did, my love.'"

"But, you already know I did."

"I know, but I still want you to say it."

"I did."

"No, say 'Yes, I did, my love.'"

"I don't really see the point."

Frustration began to build. "You will fight with a troll while it's on fire to protect me, but you won't call me your love?"

"Fighting the troll was necessary. You already know how I feel, so why do I need to say it?"

"Because you sweet and tender wife asked you to!"

"Fine! Fine! Yes I did my love. There, happy now?"

"Men!" Alice growled, turning away from him.

Sighing, Waldo admitted to himself he was glad she was feeling better. He went to where Gronk was sitting, chewing on some relatively fresh bones. "How do you feel?" Waldo put his fingers to the ogre's face, and they began to glow.

"Honestly? I'd rather poke a badger."

"Remind me to avoid these badgers. They sound as scary as rabbits."

Chapter 28

<u>Trust Is</u>

The room was empty save for a pair of torches and a single straight-backed chair. On the stone floor were two large circles, one with runes chalked on the inside, and one with them on the outside. Both magical inscriptions had been meticulously researched and chalked. Celton stood in the circle with the runes on the inside. His father was with him, seated in the chair. Both of them held their wands. Celton's heart pounded and a bead of sweat ran down the side of his face. Everything depended on tonight.

"Are the seals correct?"

"Yes, father."

"Check them again."

"I have checked them twice."

"Just do it," Dante snapped.

"Yes, Father," Celton bent over to inspect the runes. He knew they were perfect. No vampire would be able to enter the circle while they were intact.

"If this is a trick I'll burn the vampire to ashes."

"Do you really think he would come here if he wasn't serious? I am sure he knows what will happen if he lies."

"Where Lilith is concerned anything is possible."

Celton finished looking over the runes and straightened. "I am sure she would not acrifice her familiar."

"You don't know a damn thing. I have dealt with that miserable whore for close to thirty years. She is the most deceitful, clever, and ruthless person I've ever met. Nothing is beyond her." Dante clutched his wand in both hands. "Lilith is a monster."

Celton nodded.

"I am not afraid of her."

"Of course not, father, no one thinks-"

"Yes they do! Do you think I'm an idiot? I see the looks, I hear the whispers. From you, from the family, from the Council members, I know what all of you think. That woman insults me and I am forced to swallow it. Her very existence mocks me! When she's dead I'll have her head made into a drinking cup."

Just so long as someone else brings it to you. Celton was reminded of how dangerous the situation was. If things went badly they would go very bad.

His father noticed. "Nervous?"

"Not at all."

"Are you sure? If the vampire doesn't show up, or if this turns out to be a trick, it won't end well for you. Sitting with the grandchildren will be the least of your worries."

Father did love to make threats. "What happens if I succeed? If Enver comes here tonight and betrays all of Lilith's secrets?"

Dante gave an indifferent shrug. "You'll be rewarded once she is dead." Father enjoyed going into detail when it came to possible punishments. Rewards were always left ambiguous.

"Tell me something, Father. Who do you think should be your heir?"

Dante scowled. "What a pointless question. Even if everything works out perfectly, I won't name anyone. You should know that."

"I do. But we are alone. This once, tell me who you think should follow after you."

"Why? Do you expect to gain some sort of advantage once I'm gone?"

"If only once, I want to hear you acknowledge all my hard work over the years. I have done everything you have ever asked of me, all the dirty, thankless tasks you never wanted to deal with yourself. You never once gave me my due. All I ever got was more work. This one time, I want you to admit I am the one who deserves to be your heir."

"I owe you nothing." Dante sneered exposing those rotten teeth. "Don't stand there and pretend you had a choice. You did what I ordered you to. If you hadn't, you'd be dead now. I'll admit you're competent. I suppose I'll go so far to say of all my children you're the most competent. It's what's made you so useful over the years."

"Is that really all you'll give me, Father? Can't you admit I'm the most deserving?"

"Why should I?"

"Because it's the truth."

"The truth?" Dante chortled. "When has such a thing ever mattered?"

"It matters, Father, though I know you've never thought so."

"You're wrong. When you are the head of the family, you get to decide what is important and what's not."

"Then tell me, what matters to you?"

"Why are you asking me all these questions?"

"It's rare when I actually have your full attention. I want to take advantage of it."

"By asking useless questions?"

"I don't think they're useless."

Dante leaned back into his chair. "What is it you expect to hear? You know what matters to me: my pleasures, my reputation, my revenge. It's pointless to ask something when you already know the answer."

"What about the family?"

"What about them?"

"Don't we matter?"

"The ones who are useful do. The rest of you are only mouths to feed."

"Don't you care even a little bit about our House? Even if you don't love the members of it, doesn't Poisondagger matter to you?"

"I am Poisondagger."

"Only until you die. What happens to the family then?"

"I don't care. Once I'm gone, let the Dark Powers sort it all out."

Celton wasn't surprised by any of the answers. It wasn't as if his father had ever bothered to keep his opinions a secret. The fact there was no designated heir told you all you needed to know. The policy had nothing to do with being ruthless. Every head of a Great House was ruthless, but all the others named heirs for the good of their families. Father's refusal to do the same was a matter of pure selfishness. He would gladly let the House fall apart if it meant he could survive one more day.

Yet Celton felt disappointed because father wouldn't acknowledge his worth. Not even here, when they were completely alone. He really would have liked one word of thanks. But it wasn't going to come.

XXX

Not long after, a frail figure climbed through the open window. The vampire was near silent as he arrived. He gave his cape a dramatic swirl as he offered the two of them a bow. "I trust I have not kept you gentlemen waiting?"

Dante sat with his hands folded in his lap. The wand did not point at the vampire, but it remained at the ready. Celton stood directly behind his father, both of them within the circle warded against vampires.

Dante considered the vampire standing before him. The monster didn't look like much, not even in his true form. Enver seemed small and emaciated. His appearance would lead you to believe he could not be much of a threat. The vampire's reputation was something very different. In the city of Alter, he was considered the second deadliest creature alive, second only to Baldwin's familiar Zereul. It was why Dante had taken such care with the Circles. "No, you are right on time."

"I trust you have kept our meeting a secret as I requested?"

"Naturally. I know how smart Lilith is. I wouldn't risk her finding out about any of this. Even my personal guards know nothing. We three are the only ones who are aware of this meeting."

"Excellent." Enver's eyes drifted from the old man's face to the one behind him. In that instant he knew. And it was too late. He could feel the tip of his son's wand pressing against the side of his neck.

"*Telum.*"

It was a basic attack spell. One single ball of compressed mana fired out of Celton's wand. From fifteen yards away, Dante's protective wards would have dissipated it. From as close as ten, they might have still been effective. At point blank range, even the strongest protective wards were worthless.

Dante felt the spell rip out most of his throat. His mouth was filled with hot blood, drowning him. He managed to get to his feet and turn his wand on his traitorous son, but he could no longer speak. The boy knew it and stood unafraid. "It had to be this way father." He reached into one of his pockets for a dagger. "*Jacaro.*"

Dante was tossed out of the circle and landed hard on his side. He tried to stand, to take revenge, but there was no strength left. Dante collapsed and closed his eyes.

The Dark Powers would judge him.

Celton watched as his father stopped moving. The blood from his wound formed a pool around him. There was no hint of regret or guilt at what he'd done. Celton only wished he could have accomplished it ten years earlier. What flooded through him was mostly relief. "It's finally over."

"Wouldn't it be more accurate to say it's begun?" Enver made a point to step around the body without getting blood on his shoes. "This is the beginning of a new era, is it not?"

Celton nodded. "True. It's the end of the start of a new day."

"And who better to lead it than you? Celton Poisondagger, head of the Poisondagger family." Enver placed a hand over his heart and bent his neck ever so slightly.

"I'm not head yet. I still need your help with the rest of the plan. Before anyone finds out my father is dead, I need to kill the other candidates. It's unfortunate but the only way I can safely seize control."

"That is what we agreed upon. All you need do is take me to their rooms, and I will deal with them for you. I will be as swift and painless as I can."

"I only care about quick. It doesn't matter how much they suffer."

Enver chuckled. "Being around Lilith, I sometimes forget how cruel families can be."

"Really? I thought she was as cold hearted as any. The way she sacrificed her spy wasn't what I would call soft."

"Oh, she is utterly ruthless, make no mistake there. But she has surprising weak points where her own children are concerned."

He walked out of the Circle to join Enver by the door. There was no time to waste. The coup had to be over before father's body was discovered. "Please tell your mistress that once this is done and I am in control, I will keep my word. The feud between our two houses is over. She will have my full support on the Council for as long as we are both on it."

"I will tell her. You have my word."

Celton gave his father a last look. "He survived a long time, longer than he should have. He died because he trusted me, even if it was only a little."

Enver nodded. "Trusting the wrong person can have fatal consequences. After all, what is the old saying?" The vampire moved so fast Celton never saw the hand that knocked his wand away or the one that grabbed his throat and squeezed it like a vice. He clutched at the arm trying to break free, but it was like trying to bend an iron bar. Enver slammed Celton against the wall and leaned in close to whisper in his ear. "Trust is…"

There was a sudden jerk and sharp pain, followed by darkness.

XXX

Lilith waited alone in her study. She could sense her familiar's approach. Enver entered without bothering to knock and gave her one of his exaggerated bows. "Celton wanted me to tell you he planned to honor his agreement and support you on the Council so long as you were both members."

Her only reply was to raise an eyebrow.

"I promised him I would tell you that."

"I assume this promise was made before you murdered him?"

"It would have been hard to make otherwise. Unlike you, I can't summon spirits."

"I can sense how pleased you are through the bond. Does this mean everything went as planned?"

"I'm afraid so. It was almost too easy. Celton killed Dante and then I killed Celton. There were no screams and no guards."

"And you *didn't* feed, correct?"

Enver made a sour face. "No."

"Did you remember to wipe the Circles clean?" She could sense annoyance from him.

"I followed your instructions exactly."

"With no obvious evidence to the contrary, they will assume the two killed each other in a botched assassination."

"Why didn't you let Celton do it? I suspect the boy would have kept his agreement, for a while at least. He might have made a decent family head."

"He would have, that's why I wanted him dead, too. The last thing I want is someone who is actually capable in charge of Poisondagger."

XXX

Lilith didn't manage to get much sleep during the night. She found a window with a clear view of Castle Poisondagger. As it burned, she watched with delight.

Chapter 29

Fresh Start

Melissa Cornwall arrived at Norwich the following day. During her travels through Lothas, she never had reason to visit this particular city. Today was clearly not the best day to make a first impression.

The air stank of smoke. Dozens of columns of white and black smoke still rose over the city. To the right of the gate there was a large gap where some of the outer wall collapsed. From what she could see, nothing remained but charred ruins.

The city itself was not the only source of smoke.

Outside the main gate were a pair of bonfires. Carts brought out bodies. Weary men threw them one by one into the flames. By the way they shuffled back and forth as they worked, Melissa suspected these men had been at it for many hours.

Making her way here Melissa had come across a few refugees filled with wild tales about liches and armies of undead. People tended to exaggerate, especially when they were scared, but they also didn't abandon their homes for mere rumors. While finding Waldo remained her priority, Melissa decided to offer her services upon her arrival. This was just the sort of problem the Order of Mist was suited for, and it would help their reputation in this country. Sadly, she arrived too late it would seem, but she would offer what help she could while investigating if anyone had seen Waldo. Somehow she never even considered the possibility Waldo might be dead. Melissa was certain to her core that she would eventually get her hands on him.

As she approached the open gate, the men there gave her a very special welcome. The soldiers on the battlements all took out bows and nocked them. A squad of soldiers approached her with their swords out. She came to a halt and stared. Running into people who distrusted and feared her was nothing new, but they were never openly threatening. Obviously what they had gone through had shaken their wits, and they didn't understand what they were doing. Melissa stood where she was with her hands to her side. She did not take out her wand. A few calming words would ease their fears. Then she would meet the local lord and find out how she could help.

"What do you want?" The sergeant in charge asked.

Despite his tone Melissa dipped her head graciously. "My name is Melissa Cornwall of the Order of Mist. I wish upon you the blessings of Unity, Justice, and Peace. I desire to speak with your lord and offer him whatever aid I can."

"Duke Griffinheart wants no help from your kind."

She was surprised at how blatant the hostility was. Even kings would at least try and disguise how they felt. "I know there are many stories and rumors about White Mages, but most of them are idle gossip. We seek only to help people."

"Liar," one of the soldiers spat. The sergeant nodded.

"Whatever you might believe, it's for your lord to decide whether or not to accept my help. Can one of you guide me to him?"

"You are not going to meet with the duke."

"Forgive me, but I don't think it is your decision to make."

"It's the duke's orders. No White Mages are permitted to enter Norwich."

Melissa's eyes widened. "You are barring us? My entire order? Does your lord understand how offensive his command is?"

"Not as offensive as stealing his ancestral blade or summoning an army of undead to attack us."

"What?"

"One of your sort was here and was the duke's guest, him and his two women. He summoned a horde of evil abominations and stole our lord's magical sword before they arrived."

"The alligation is ridiculous and beyond insulting! We are not common thieves, and summoning undead is an act of blasphemy! No White Mage would ever do such a thing!"

"We all saw him with his red haired woman and savage. The lich even admitted to being summoned by him. I heard it with my own ears."

The soldiers all nodded.

With the mention of a red haired woman, Melissa got a sickening feeling in the pit of her stomach.

"The person who did all this, his name wouldn't have been Waldo Rabbit would it?"

"So you know him."

Melissa looked at the bonfires being fed bodies, the ruined section of wall, and at the smoke still rising above the city. *How could one man cause so much harm? It's been less than two weeks!* When word of this spread, it would cause more damage to her order than a hundred false rumors. She was sorely tempted to tell the sergeant the truth. Waldo was not really a White Mage. But she could not. Her instructions from Minster Barrows were explicit on that point. It wasn't likely the truth would be believed anyway. Under the circumstances, it would sound too much like a lie of convenience. "I know him, though I am beginning to suspect I know him less than I thought."

"Then you should know Duke Griffinheart has declared that until Waldo Rabbit is returned to face trial for his crimes, no White Mage will be permitted to step inside Norwich."

"You cannot put a member of my order on trial. Local lords have no authority over us." It was bizarre to be defending someone she knew was not actually a White Mage. The principle was what needed to be defended, though. If one petty nobleman could actually put a White Mage on trial it would set a dangerous precedent.

"Maybe it's time for things to change. You whites act like small gods. You should answer for your crimes like anyone else."

Melissa's back stiffened. She was not used to being spoken to this way. "We serve a higher purpose. We cannot be constrained by archaic laws or petty local authorities."

"Yeah, you do whatever you please," one of the soldiers said. "It's why no one trusts your kind."

"Everyone knows you keep secrets," a third soldier said.

It was the same problem as always. Her order fought for the greater good. Which often required committing small evils. People couldn't understand because they could never see beyond their own self-interests. "Whatever your duke believes, he is making a grave mistake. Kings and queens welcome us. We can travel anywhere we please in the Shattered Lands, except to Alteroth. If he truly means to bar us from his city, there will be consequences."

The sergeant raised his sword a few inches and widened his stance. His men spread out. "If you want to try and ignore my lord's order, you will regret it, white."

Melissa shook her head. "I will not. If it is your duke's will for me to be turned away, I shall go, but please inform him that his decision will not be forgotten."

Though it galled her, Melissa had no choice but to leave.

XXX

Lancel and his men arrived two days later.

On his way, he'd come across some villagers who'd been fleeing south. The story they'd told sounded ridiculous. Liches and skeletons and walking corpses were the stuff of children's stories. Maybe they existed beyond the border where the black wizards ruled but not here. Passing through his first empty village with desecrated graves, he began to wonder. When he saw his third, he put his horse into a gallop.

Unlike Melissa, he and his men were welcomed when they finally arrived. The soldiers at the gate cheered him and were quick to report his father was wounded but not severely. They also told they really had been attacked by an army of undead led by a lich. There was also something about a White Mage who stole Lawgiver and summoned the abominations in the first place. The latter sounded even more outlandish than the tale of an army of undead storming through the countryside.

The sight of the broken wall was hard to accept. Like everyone else in Norwich, he never doubted the strength of these walls. Seeing a section of them ripped down made him wonder what other false assumptions he held. Almost as unsettling were the pair of bonfires and the wagonload of rotting corpses being carted out to them. The dead were supposed to be buried, not burned like trash. The sergeant in charge told him it was his father's orders. They did not know exactly how many had been killed, but the number was staggering, perhaps as high as three thousand. Some of the old stories said those killed by the dead would rise as well. His father could not know for certain but would take no chances. The departed who had not been consumed when Norwich burned would go into these fires. All the corpses were to be destroyed.

As Lancel and his men rode in through the gate, a couple families were leaving: two women and a total of seven children of different ages. They carried nothing but the clothes on their back. They were returning to their village and would try to rebuild it and bring in some crops. The task would be very hard for them, especially with no men to help.

He felt some sympathy for them until he entered the city.

Half of it was nothing but blackened ruin. Entire miles were piles of charred wood and stone. The smell of smoke and rot flavored every breath. He could see people going through the destruction, searching for something to salvage or perhaps for the remains of loved ones. Along the street, many hungry faces covered in soot begged for alms. He reached into his purse and tossed some silver coins. Lancel was careful not to waste any of the gold.

How many years would it take to repair all this? Would they still be recovering when he was duke? How much would it cost? He was glad this wasn't his worry. Financial responsibility fell squarely on his father. Lancel would help in any way he could, this was home after all, but hopefully his services would not be needed for too long.

The keep was untouched and exactly as he remembered, except for the number of guards surrounding it. All the soldiers recognized him and looked pleased at his return. Lancel had his men stable the horses and then find rooms for themselves, as he sought his father. Sir Lancel found him in his quarters, most of his right arm was wrapped in cloth dressings.

"Father." Lancel immediately embraced the old man.

"Son." With his good hand, Theos lightly patted his son's shoulder.

Lancel was surprised at both his father's distant tone and expression. Given the recent events, he'd expected a much warmer welcome.

"Are you all right, Father?"

Theos took a couple steps away from him. "If you mean this, I am fine." The duke bent and unbent the injured arm. "If you mean the city, I am anything but. Many lost everything and have nowhere to sleep. The food stores are burnt. I have ordered all those who came here from the countryside back. The fields were burned and the farm animals slaughtered, I don't know what sort of crop they will be able to bring in. With them gone, there are fewer mouths, but how are we to feed them all? Many of the ones who are still alive will starve come the winter. If we are still alive come the winter. As soon as the goblins know our walls are broken, they are going to march and attack us, nothing surer." Theos stared out a window at his ruined city.

"Maybe I am cursed," he muttered, barely loud enough for Lancel to hear. "Maybe the wizard really did steal my luck."

"A wizard?" A few came through on occasion, usually hedge wizards selling potions or offering to make it rain. The powerful ones never had reason to visit such an out of the way place. "I heard some bizarre story about a White Mage who stole Lawgiver and summoned the lich and his army."

"Sadly, it's a true tale, my son. Lawgiver was stolen from me by a cowardly white named Waldo Rabbit."

Waldo? "Why would a White Mage do something so despicable?"

"Who can guess? They are full of secrets and deceptions. But there is more you might like to know, my son. He didn't come here alone. He brought two women with him, and one of them was yours."

"He had Lucilla with him?"

"No! Not your useless wife! He had your woman, the barmaid Alice."

Lancel sucked in a breath and had to bite back the urge to yell a denial. Since burning down the damned whorehouse, he wanted to forget Alice ever existed. "You must be mistaken, Father. It had to be some other wench with the same name."

"There was no mistake. It would be hard to confuse her with anyone else. Long red hair, violet eyes, and tits big enough to use as pillows. She even admitted to knowing you."

Alice coming here and actually meeting his father was the worst possible scenario. If his father learned the truth, Lancel would be disgraced and disowned. "Whatever she told you was a damned lie. She's nothing but a common whore, and I have never lain with her nor wanted to."

"Your words now are the lies. You went on and on about her. It's how I knew who she was at first sight. And I'll admit she is quite a woman. I can understand why you wanted her so badly."

"Perhaps I did want her once, but I lost interest. She is nothing special to me at all."

His father gave him a condescending look. "What? Does it bother you how this wizard snapped her up before you could? He actually married her, you know, or so they said. He had her and an ugly brute of a woman, too."

This doesn't make any sense. Alice came here with a White Mage? How is such a thing even possible? She's a monster, and she was even in the company of a dark wizard before he was killed.

The answer was obvious, and it came to him as soon as the initial shock passed. Was it really possible the same Dark Mage who originally met her back in Stratford somehow didn't drown and actually came here as a *guest*? The idea of not only a monster but a black wizard staying here and fooling his father was sickening. The only thing worse was if his father realized the truth. Lancel was connected to Alice in the duke's eyes. Any sort of tie between him and a monster or dark mage would be enough to ruin him.

"It was Alice who actually took Lawgiver from me." His father was trying to sound stern, but there was a touch of longing in his voice. "She bewitched me. She was waiting at my door and pleaded with me to give her my sword. I could not refuse her." Theos shook his head as if to banish the image. "It must have been her idea to come here. Why else would a White Mage visit? If you had never encountered the woman, none of this would ever have happened."

"Father, you can't blame me for what she or this wizard did."

"Maybe not directly, but your actions still brought all this misfortune down on us. Perhaps the gods are punishing me for my pride or you for yours, but one thing is clear to me. From the moment I lost possession of Lawgiver, our family's luck has been poisoned. I am sure the only way to get our luck back is for you to go on a quest to recover our ancestral sword."

"How am I to do so when they have disappeared with no trace?"

"You will have to track them or plead with the gods for a sign. In any case, my son, you *will* go on this quest, and you will not return without Lawgiver. If you can return Waldo here to face my judgment, he and his order will answer for his crimes. But returning the blade is what truly matters."

Lancel could have told his father the White Mages had nothing to do with any of it. But saying so would have required him to explain, and the truth was the last thing he needed. "What happens if I cannot find Alice or this Waldo?"

"Then you will never return home, never become duke, and never take my place. Set your mind to it, Lancel. You succeed on your quest, or you lose everything."

This was completely and utterly unjust, but Lancel could not refuse. "I understand, Father."

Three days following their encounter with the troll. The four of them had finally made it out of the marshes and were walking through the green hill country of Umbria. They'd spotted a few shepherds and flocks of sheep in the distance but had yet to actually run into any of the natives. The four of them had protective wards placed on themselves. Gronk was Belle again, and he, Alice, and Waldo were all completely healed.

As they went, Waldo reached into one of the many hidden pockets of his robe and took out a hunk of blackish brown meat. He held it to his mouth and worked to bite off a piece, then slowly chewed.

"How can you stand to eat that?" Cleptus asked.

Waldo swallowed. "You don't like jerky?"

"Not when it came off of a goblin."

"It's a little chewy but not bad."

"I agree with Master. Anyway, you should never waste food." Gronk was munching on a porcupine.

Cleptus shook his head.

Alice walked at her husband's side and placed a hand on his arm. "I'm sorry we weren't able to capture the troll, darling. I know how important it was to you."

"It's fine. Having you and Gronk is more than enough. I am glad to have you both."

"Still, I know getting him was part of your quest."

"I only need three monsters as familiars, they don't have to be Great Monsters. When the time comes, all I need to do is make a goblin or orc a familiar to fulfill the first part of my quest." He glanced back at Cleptus and lowered his voice. "The other parts are what I'm worried about." Waldo intended to use the thief, but was not going to trust him. So far as Cleptus was concerned, Waldo really was a White Mage on some vague, unexplained mission.

"I'm sure you'll figure it out, darling, and you know I'll help you in any way I can."

He grinned at her. "So long as it doesn't involve me asking you to use your Charm, steal, take slaves, or do anything else against your high morals."

She nodded and looked very pleased. There was a pulse of happiness from the bond. "See? You're learning."

"I am. Almost everything I've come across since setting out has been a new experience. I've even killed for the very first time."

"Was it hard for you, darling? It didn't seem to bother you."

"Actually it wasn't. I didn't think about it. I simply did what I had to. Mother always said killing was easy so long as you didn't care about your victim."

Alice gave him a wide smile. "Very evil of you."

"Thank you." Waldo looked at the vast horizon before him and felt at ease. Even the terrible ball of fire overhead did not bother him... much. "Lothas is behind us, the world in front of us, today is a fresh start, and all things are possible. Grandfather will still be chasing us and maybe Melissa as well, but we'll deal with them when we have to."

"So I get to travel all over the Shattered Lands with you having adventures?" She slid her arm through his. "I like the sound of that."

"Good. I certainly wouldn't want to try and manage without you."

Alice leaned in close and deliberately let her breasts rub against his arm.

"You know, darling," she said in a throaty whisper. "The first town we come to with an inn we should stay the night."

"All right. After camping in the grass and mud I wouldn't mind sleeping in a real bed again."

"Yes, and we could, ah, *make the bed together*." She added a purr to those last few words.

"If we're paying for a room at an inn, shouldn't the bed already be made?"

"Uhm, not really what I meant."

Waldo looked unsure. "Then what did you mean?"

"You know, the thing we do in bed together."

"Sleep?"

"No, the other thing."

"You mean how you try to crush me as I sleep?"

"No!"

Waldo paused and rubbed his chin. "Do you mean when I service you?"

Alice let go of him and rubbed her temples. "Yes, and do you have to say it in such a crude way?"

"Why would you want us to make the bed when we're going to make a mess of the sheets anyway?"

"Never mind. I suddenly have a headache." Alice picked up her pace and was soon ahead of everyone else.

From their connection, Waldo knew he somehow managed to upset her again. It was all right. He was still learning, after all.

He bit off another piece of goblin jerky and hummed to himself.

The world awaited.

THE END

Made in the USA
Lexington, KY
15 March 2017